About the author

Stewart Cant was born in Salisbury, Southern Rhodesia (now Harare, Zimbabwe) and currently lives in Johannesburg, South Africa. He is married and has two sons from a previous marriage, both of whom live in the USA. Stewart is a semi-retired legal consultant, specialising in drafting legal documents in plain English.

*AUTO*BIOGRAPHY:

My Life Story through Motor Vehicles.

Stewart Cant

*AUTO*BIOGRAPHY:
My Life Story through Motor Vehicles.

Vanguard Press

VANGUARD PAPERBACK

A CIP catalogue record for this title is
available from the British Library.

ISBN 978 1 784654 12 2

Vanguard Press is an imprint of
Pegasus Elliot MacKenzie Publishers Ltd.
www.pegasuspublishers.com

First Published in 2018

Vanguard Press
Sheraton House Castle Park
Cambridge England

Printed & Bound in Great Britain

Dedication

To my wife, Sherryl.

Chapter 1
INTRODUCTION

I was thinking about the various cars I have owned over the years and it struck me that motor vehicles have been such an integral part of my life that much of my life story could be told through them (an *auto*biography). On land: cars and motorbikes of every description, as well as trains and buses and other motorised vehicles. On water: all sorts of boats and ships. In the air: a variety of aircraft from a microlight to Jumbo jets.

It also strikes me that I have lived through the heyday of petrol and diesel engines – now that we are moving into an era of electric motors. There is irony in the fact that a number of my ancestors were blacksmiths in the days of horse drawn transport. I was born in 1951, along with the BMW 501, the Ford Consul, the Mercedes-Benz W187 and the Volvo Titan, to name a few. During my childhood, in what was then Southern Rhodesia, big American V8s were all the rage. Then came a lot of British cars and motorbikes, my dream car in my late teens being the E- Type Jaguar. Also cars from other parts of Europe: German, Italian and French cars stand out in my memory. After that, of course, Japanese cars and bikes came to dominate in most segments, except for supercars where Germany and Italy continue to be at the forefront.

Chapter 2
My Family

DAD

My love of motor vehicles, especially sports cars, comes from my Dad.

Charlie Cant was born in 1920 in Edinburgh, Scotland. He qualified as a Motor Engineer (motor mechanic in modern parlance). Soon after the outbreak of the Second World War, he volunteered to join the Royal Air Force and commenced training to become a pilot. However, when the RAF discovered he was a qualified motor mechanic, he was transferred to aircraft maintenance – to his great and lasting disappointment.

Whilst serving at a Forward Air Field in Malaya, the Japanese invaded. My father spoke very little about his wartime experiences, but I do remember him telling me that he and some of his RAF comrades hijacked a steam train and tried to escape their Japanese pursuers. They were captured sometime during 1942 and Charlie spent the rest of the war as a Japanese prisoner of war. I have "Christmas menus" (which, I understand, were done as tongue-in-cheek wish lists); one marked 'Lyceum Camp, Soerabaya 1942' and the other

'Pangkalin, Balai, Sumatra 1943'. I remember Dad saying that the cartoonist and author, Ronald Searle, was a fellow POW and I think Dad said it was Searle who drew up the menus. I know that Dad ended up in Changi prison in Singapore. Having read a number of books written by Japanese POWs, I know something of the horrors Dad endured. Despite that, he had nothing against the ordinary people in Malaya and Singapore – even the Japanese. He said the locals were often kind, passing gifts of food through the camp fence at great risk to themselves. Most of the Japanese guards, however, were evil and unnecessarily cruel. Unlike their compatriots in German prison camps, escape was not an option for Allied troops in Japanese prison camps: Europeans on a peninsula or an island in the Far East had nowhere to hide and nowhere to go. By the time Charlie was liberated at the end of the War, he was suffering from beriberi which causes severe bloating.

Following his recovery in hospital and discharge from the Air Force, he received a letter from King George sent to all liberated Japanese prisoners of war (which I still have). I believe that was the extent of the thanks he received. No monetary compensation from the Japanese or British Governments for his suffering. In 2000 (many years after his death), the British Government paid compensation of ten thousand GBP to each remaining survivor and, in the case of my father, to my mother as his widow. My mother kindly shared this amount with my brother and me. I used some of my share to buy a signet ring identical to one my father used to wear, which I wear all the time as a memento.

Dad married my mother, Marion Stewart, in 1949 in Penicuik, Scotland. He had been on a troop ship which called at Cape Town during the War and he and Mum looked into emigrating from Scotland to South Africa. At that time, the British Government was offering assisted passage to immigrants to Southern Rhodesia so they took that option, travelling by ship to Cape Town and then by train to Salisbury in Southern Rhodesia early in 1950. I was born in 1951 and my brother, Chris Cant, was born in 1953. Dad was employed in various motor mechanic related capacities. I remember him bringing home a variety of company owned and badged small trucks, in the open back of which my brother and I would be taken for rides (illegal these days but not then). At times I am sure Dad saw me as a real pain: he frequented a few "watering holes", in particular the Sherwood Arms Hotel and the Drill Hall pub which was for current and ex-servicemen. He would collect Chris and me from school, or wherever, and call in for a couple of beers. We would be left in the car and he would buy us Cokes and crisps and I would complain that we wanted to go home and would tell Mum if he didn't hurry up – then I regret that I often would do so and be responsible for an argument between my parents.

Dad was definitely a 'petrol head' (although that is a term not used back then), but had a number of disappointments related to motor vehicles. I have already mentioned the first; not being allowed to complete training as a pilot. On holiday in Durban when my brother and I were kids, he took us for a flip in a small plane and told us he would have loved to be able to fly the plane himself. Given the death rate of pilots in the War, I guess my brother and I may owe our existence to Dad's misfortune. Another misfortune related to vintage cars. Dad helped an older friend of his to restore two vintage cars on the agreement that one of them would be bequeathed to Dad. Unfortunately, after the friend's death, his wife denied any knowledge of this arrangement and sold both the cars. Dad was also keen on motor racing and took my brother and me to watch various types of races at the Marlborough track in Salisbury. I know he would have loved to race himself, but again, his only involvement was as a mechanic. I also know that he would have loved to own a sports car, particularly an MG TF. Unfortunately he never had the opportunity nor had the chance to enjoy the string of sports cars my brother and I have owned over the years.

My parents, brother and I spent three years at Mangula Mine in Rhodesia, during which Chris and I had happy times, but I now know that our parents had some problems. I remember Dad doing fun things like taking us for drives in trucks and graders and on holidays to Beira in Mozambique, but generally it was Mum who brought us up. Towards the end of our time in Mangula, I was often kept awake at night by arguments between my parents. Only many years later did Mum tell me that Dad was eventually fired from his job as Transport Manager due to problems with alcohol. We moved back to Salisbury and Dad had a couple of jobs as a mechanic with small workshops. He got a position as a Quality Control Manager at the Ford Motor Company's car assembly plant in Rhodesia and it appears that he managed to get his life and marriage back on track. I remember doing a junior school project on "My Father's Job." My then best friend Peter Saker's father worked for Land Rover and he and I got top marks for our projects on Land Rover and Ford respectively. Towards the end of 1964, there was family discussion about a planned move to South America, where my father was to assist in opening a new Ford assembly plant. However, one day early in 1965, Dad came off the soccer field and coughed up some blood. He was diagnosed as having lung cancer. He had one lung removed and underwent chemo and radio therapy. The planned move to South America did not happen. I sometimes think about how twists of fate determine the remainder of one's life. Imagine how different my future would have been if we had moved to South America when I was in my early teens.

As Dad's condition continued to deteriorate, he decided to stop treatment and stay at home instead of remaining in hospital. He spent most of his time in bed, sedated by strong painkillers, and from time to time using an iron lung to assist his breathing. I do remember him getting out of bed to help with putting up Christmas decorations. He had been a big man (six foot tall and well built), but was by then a shrivelled husk. Dad died in the early hours of Christmas morning on 25 December, 1965 at just forty-five years of age. He had been a heavy smoker which probably caused his death, although we did wonder whether the malnutrition and other diseases he suffered in POW camps had a contributory effect.

MUM

My mother, Marion Harwood (born Stewart, previously Cant), was not a car person, but she was a good driver and taught my brother and me to drive. I remember accusing her of deliberately having a spring in her neck, because whenever I hit the brake, her head would shoot forwards and when I accelerated, it shot backwards.

Mum had a variety of ordinary sedan cars over the years. After Dad's death, my brother and I tried to persuade her to buy a sports car and nearly succeeded, but she ended up with another sedan. She did at one time buy a Velosolex, which is like a bicycle with a motor that drops onto the front wheel. A friend's mother also had one and I remember having drag races by revving the motor to its maximum before dropping it onto the front wheel (unbeknown to our mothers).

Mum was a schoolteacher and years after my father's death, she moved to Bulawayo, Rhodesia to take up a post as a lecturer at the Teacher's Training College. There she met, dated and married a fellow lecturer, George Harwood. He was a divorced Englishman with a full beard and twinkling blue eyes. He was likeable, interesting and somewhat eccentric. He had been a navigator in a Mosquito aeroplane during the Second World War. Mum and George moved to Durban, South Africa during 1977, where Mum took up the position of Headmistress of Durban Girls College, an exclusive private senior school for girls. George obtained a post as a lecturer at the University of Natal (Durban). Marion and George retired to Kendal in the UK. By this time, Mum's younger son and one of George's daughters were living with their families in Perth, Western Australia. After visiting a few times, Marion and George bought a house in Perth and embarked on an enviable lifestyle – spending the Northern Hemisphere summer in Kendal and winter in Perth. They also travelled extensively, coming out to Southern Africa on a number of occasions, as well as visiting the US, Russia and many countries in Europe. Clearly, they had money to enable them to do all this, but they still lived frugally, with jalopies for cars, economy class travel, and what appeared to be a tight budget. For example, I remember being on holiday in Australia with them and my brother and his family. On a number of occasions the rest of us dined in style in a restaurant while they ate sandwiches on a bench on the beach, declining our offers to pay for them. We knew they had good pensions and thought that they lived as they did in order to be able to afford all the travelling. Imagine our surprise to later discover that George had been a shrewd investor on the stock market and that, towards the end of their lives, they were much wealthier than their lifestyle suggested.

Marion and George were both amazingly fit. I remember hiking for miles in the hills of the Lake District with them as recently as 2007 (by which time Marion was seventy-eight and George was eighty-three). Sadly, George developed breathing problems and Marion arthritis and they realised that they could not continue their nomadic lifestyle. In 2009, they decided to move permanently to Perth. However, a week before they were due to fly they had to cancel as Marion fell and broke her femur, after which her physical and mental health deteriorated rapidly. Sherryl and I visited them during July 2010 and they had moved into sheltered housing in a rented council owned flat in Kendal. After we returned to South Africa, we were advised by George's son that George had been admitted to hospital with fluid in his lungs and Marion had been put into a temporary care home.

George died on 15 October, 2010. An autopsy revealed the cause of death to have been Asbestosis. My wife, Sherryl, and I and my brother and his wife, flew to the UK to be with Mum. By this time she was in Summerhill Nursing and Care Home in Kendal. We soon realised that she was not receiving the treatment she needed. She was in a room in the secured section for advanced Alzheimer's patients. Although she obviously had this condition and was only lucid from time to time, her physical condition was worse than her mental state: she was skin and bone, covered in bruises from falling and clearly in a lot of pain. Despite this, the caregivers were getting her out of bed, washed, dressed and fed every morning and she believed she would get into trouble if she went back to bed. Thank goodness that we went over, as it emerged that, despite knowing that she had Alzheimer's disease and suspected stomach cancer (which none of the family, except perhaps her late husband, knew about) her National Health Service doctor had not seen her in more than a month. We managed to arrange for her to be seen by another doctor, her own doctor, and the district nurse, and to be put onto four core drugs and palliative care for the terminally ill. She had a living will and nothing was done to keep her alive, just to make her more comfortable. Mum told us that she wanted to be with George, but at the same time she seemed to believe that she had an obligation to hold onto life. I told her that, if she was ready to go, she should do so. Sherryl and I bid her farewell on a Friday evening as we had to return to South Africa the next day. We were with Chris and Trish later that evening in the pub at which we were staying when we received the news that Marion had passed away. She died on 23 October, 2010, just a week after the death of her beloved husband George.

GRAN

An important member of our family during my childhood was my maternal grandmother, Christina Stewart. She was born in North Berwick, Scotland on 11 October, 1900, the same year as the Queen Mother, to whom, at least in their later years, she bore a strong resemblance. Gran grew up in interesting times, seeing the first motor cars and aeroplanes and living through two World Wars. Surprisingly, she never obtained a driver's license – in fact, never even tried to drive a car as far as I know.

Gran's husband died in 1945 and she followed my parents, emigrating from Scotland to Salisbury, Southern Rhodesia early in 1951. She was the sort of grandmother any child would like to have: kind and homely, with a variety of interests which included cooking, baking, sewing, knitting, growing pot plants (especially African violets, some of which she would give a different colour by adding tea leaves to the soil) and birdwatching. I remember one of the jokes she told my brother and me when we were kids: "A young man came to visit his grandmother at the old age home, driving his big, new V8. He took his Gran and several other old ladies for a fast drive. When they got back, he said to his Gran,

"Some speed eh?"

His Gran replied, "Some's peed, some's pooed and some's passed right out."

Gran ended up in an old age home in Durban, South Africa, where I visited her on a couple of occasions, but did not take her and her friends for a drive! She died in 1983 and I went with my mother to formally identify the body; this was the first time that I had seen a dead person and it was hard to believe Gran was gone because it looked as if she was asleep.

BROTHER

My younger brother, Chris Cant, is also something of a "petrol head". Unlike me, he is not only interested in motor vehicles, but also has the ability to tinker with them and to repair them. I picked up all the jargon: "skimmed heads", "banana bunch exhaust", "double overhead cam" and so on, so I sound knowledgeable, but Chris really was, and is, knowledgeable about motor vehicles. I remember being on holiday at Kariba Dam in Rhodesia on one occasion. The outboard motor on our speedboat seized and put the piston through the block. No problem for Chris and his friend Bimbo Westland. They stripped the motor on the lake shore, bought some new parts and had it running within a few hours.

Shortly after his 16th birthday, Chris bought a Matchless 500 cc motorcycle and converted it into a smart Chopper. I often borrowed his bike and have vivid memories of kick starting it – back then, bikes did not have electric starters and, as a single stroke motor, it often kicked back, on one occasion sending a friend who had borrowed it over the handlebars. I had a new pair of Italian winkle picker shoes with leather soles, which kept slipping off the starter pedal, until it kicked back and cut through the side of the shoe bruising my foot at the same time. On one occasion, I rode the bike all the way from what was then Salisbury, Rhodesia (now Harare, Zimbabwe) to Bulawayo, a distance of about four hundred and thirty kilometres. After a party the night before, I had missed my flight to Bulawayo and had to get there that day for a reason I no longer remember. But I do remember being saddle sore after the long ride.

Chris subsequently bought a Yamaha 250 cc motorbike, on which he nearly killed himself. At the time, he was working as an engineer for Rhodesian Television and lived in a mess (now known as a commune, but then more appropriately named) in Highlands, Salisbury with a number of friends, most of whom also worked for RTV. They heard Chris racing his bike through the winding road leading home and then silence. He was discovered in a culvert having taken a corner too fast, dropped the bike and slid across the road into the culvert; in the process ripping most of the skin off one side of his body and suffering concussion. He was in intensive care in hospital for a few days, but fortunately survived without any permanent damage.

That ended Chris's foray into motorbikes. He went on to have a variety of cars, starting with a white MGA, then a red MGB and later a white Alfa Romeo Spyder. I have fond memories of being at Kariba with him and some friends, including Rich Barlow, who had won a big prize in the Rhodesian State Lottery and had bought himself a new BMW. Chris and I were in the Alfa, with Rich and others behind us in the BMW, racing through the hilly curves going up to the Kariba village. We had all had lots of beers and I (stupidly with the benefit of hindsight) stood up in the open top Alfa and gave the others a brown eye. On the same visit, Chris and I (sober on this occasion) saw a pink hippo! It was walking along the roadside, clearly having wallowed in red mud.

Much to my dismay, Chris and his wife Trish, with her two sons from a previous marriage, emigrated from Zimbabwe to Perth, Australia in 1981. There, they have had a variety of cars and boats, including a Triumph Stag sports car and several speedboats – most of which I have had the pleasure of riding in during visits to Oz. On an early visit with my then teenage sons Adam and Chris, we camped at a local dam and had a lot of fun boating and water skiing. On a later visit, we spent a particularly enjoyable day in Chris's speedboat cruising along the Swan River and having lunch at Caversham Wine Estate.

After Chris was retrenched from Channel 5 television station in Perth, he and his wife started their own business operating the big screens at stadium functions, in particular the "footy" at Subiaco. To augment their seasonal income, they bought and operated a parasailing boat. I still have a voucher for a free parasail which they sent me for my fortieth birthday, but unfortunately I did not have an opportunity to use it before they sold the boat.

Chapter 3
MY FORMATIVE YEARS

I was born on 28 November, 1951 in the Lady Chancellor Nursing Home in what was then Salisbury, Southern Rhodesia (now Harare, Zimbabwe). My first home was a small-holding called Eldorado, on the outskirts of Salisbury, which was rented by my parents. I'm told that it was also nearly my last home, as my father was alerted by the barking of his Red Setter that a snake was circling my pram in the garden.

I have a photograph of me aged two or three, "helping" my father to fix his car. Also, one of me "fixing" the wheel of the pram in which my Gran was pushing my younger brother, Chris. Observers may have thought I was destined to become a mechanic or an engineer, but nothing could be further from the truth – my interest in things mechanical was not matched by any understanding or ability.

Not all my experiences with motor vehicles have been pleasant. When I was about four years old, I was in a group of children playing on a "bakkie" (a small truck with an open back) when one of the others gave me a shove and I fell off and broke my right arm.

My independent memories (not from photos) start from the age of five. My first girlfriend was a girl of the same age called Lindsay Fenn, who lived on the same street. I remember that she had ginger hair, freckles and pebble thick specs. I met her once about twelve years later and could not believe it was the same girl – by then an attractive blonde with no noticeable freckles and contact lenses. I also remember Lindsay and I setting off by bus for our first day at Alfred Beit Primary School in Mabelreign, Salisbury.

When I was about halfway through KG 2 (second year at junior school), my father got a new job as Transport Manager at Mangula Copper Mine (one hundred and twenty kilometres north-west of Salisbury) and the family moved into a mine-supplied house there. For the next three years, my brother and I attended, and my mother taught at, Mangula Primary School. Chris and I took part in the usual school and extramural sports and other activities, but had the advantage of growing up in "the bush". Outside school, like other Mangula children, we spent most of our time barefooted with the result that we developed resistant pads on our feet – resistant to most things except the occasional serious thorn or drawing pin!

Right across the road from our house was a large tract of vacant bush, with a kopje (rocky hill) and an old quarry filled with water. We spent a lot of time there, exploring and playing on foot and bicycle. I was generally a bit of a 'goody-goody,' but remember getting into big trouble there on two occasions. Once, for swimming in the bilharzia infested water of the quarry, and once when we were caught smoking cigarettes on the kopje with the garden boy (who was a teenager, but in colonial Africa even adult male household servants were referred to as "boy.") Our house boy, Fibion, (who was in his early 20s) was tasked with looking after Chris and me when neither of our parents were at home. He was amazingly tolerant, and, in addition to his household duties, he used to do things like build push-carts for us, play games with us, fix punctures on our bikes and teach us something of the customs and language (including swear words) of the Shona people. Fibion and the gardener lived in a kia (a small and very basic house) in the back garden. Unbeknown to our parents, Chris and I sometimes squatted around a fire with them and shared a meal of sadza (thick mealie meal porridge) scooped up by hand and dipped in gravy with some 'boys' meat' (which was very low quality meat).

My parents became friendly with various farmers in the neighbourhood, resulting in lots of visits to farms which are fun places for children. Happy memories include Christmas lunches, during which we were entertained by tribal dancing by the farm workers; and being driven around standing on the back of bakkies. One serious incident also stands out in my memory. A group of children including my brother and I were playing on a farm near Karoi and one or more of us threw stones into a large beehive in a tree. Swarms of angry African bees attacked anything that moved, killing chickens and a dog. We were all covered in bees and stung many times before an elderly farmworker got us into the homestead, where we took refuge under mosquito nets while bees and their stings were removed by the adults. The farmworker and one of the children had to be taken to hospital. Fortunately we all survived, having learned a valuable lesson about interfering with nature.

When I was about halfway through Standard3 (fifth year at junior school), my parents announced suddenly that we were moving back to Salisbury. Having made a lot of friends in Mangula and become accustomed to the lifestyle there, Chris and I were not happy with this, but obviously had no say in the matter. The family moved back to the lower middle-class suburb of Mabelreign in Salisbury and Chris and I were enrolled at the newish Hallingbury Primary School. I remember at the pre-enrolment interview, the Headmaster commented to my mother that we would have to wear shoes to school – much to her embarrassment she had not noticed that we had gone out barefooted!

During childhood our main form of transport was bicycles. Motorised transport was as a passenger, although my father sometimes used to let us sit on his lap and steer the car and later also demonstrated to my brother and me how to do things like a controlled drift. We loved anything we could drive ourselves: dinky cars, the amazing wire cars with steering wheels made by some African teenagers, Scalextric race cars and later tractors and motorbikes on farms and dodgem cars and go-karts.

In my last year at Junior School in 1963 my mother, grandmother, brother and I went to the UK for the whole of the second school term and had a wonderful holiday. We travelled by train to Cape Town and on the Cape Town Castle mail ship to Southampton (via Las Palmas). My mother took delivery of a new fire engine red (the colour chosen by my brother and me) Ford Cortina in London, in which we travelled around England and Scotland sightseeing and visiting relatives Chris and I had not met. An occasion which stands out is when

Chris and I went with English cousins of around the same age to take the real *'Ferry across the Mersey'* (also a hit tune at the time). We travelled by bus which they jumped off while it was still moving. I watched what they did and with some trepidation did the same. But Chris jumped off facing backward instead of forward and so fell flat on his face; fortunately the only damage was to his ego. Mum, being a schoolteacher, gave us daily lessons and we had to keep a diary of our experiences. We travelled home on the Athlone Castle mail ship (via Madeira) and my father met us at the Salisbury Railway Station.

I turned sixteen in November, 1967, and obtained my motorcycle and car drivers licenses soon thereafter. *My first motor vehicle* was a second-hand dark red Kawasaki 125 cc motorbike, which I persuaded my mother to let me buy although my father had said we would not be allowed to have motorbikes. My brother and many of our friends also had motorbikes so I had the opportunity to ride a variety of road bikes and scramblers.

My first car (*shared* with my brother,) was a pale green second-hand Fiat 500 with retractable soft top that Chris and I bought together in 1968. We had lots of fun in that car, although it often had to be push started. When either of us was on our own, he or I would park on a downhill slope, push the car from the driver's side, jump in, engage gear and drop the clutch. On one memorable occasion, Chris and I were together in the car and saw flames and smoke coming out of the bonnet – that being where the petrol tank was located, we stopped urgently and dived out of the vehicle. No explosion, but the wiring did burn out. Around this time, a neighbour who was nearer to my parents' age invited me to navigate for him in rallies. He had two cars that he used for rallying: a Rover 90 and a hotted-up Renault Gordini (which, for some reason to do with the tuning, reached its maximum speed in third gear). I enjoyed participating in a few rallies as navigator, but would have preferred to have done the driving.

I wrote the GCE 'O' level exams at the end of 1967 and managed to pass six subjects (including Maths for which I think I must have been given someone else's mark). The following two years during which I studied for the GCE 'A' level exams were somewhat different. The 'A' level classes from Ellis Robins Boys High (which I attended), Mount Pleasant Boys High and Mabelreign Girls High were combined and we travelled by bus from Ellis Robins to Mount Pleasant for our classes. I chose English, French and History as my subjects and the classes were much less structured than they had been up to then. I made some new friends and became a bit of a rebel from the school system. I was not into rugby or cricket and therefore not part of the 'in crowd'. My achievements in drama, debating, public speaking and extramural horse riding and sailing did not help and I was not selected as a prefect. I got into a lot of non-school activities like smoking, drinking, playing drums in a band, playing pinball and mini soccer at cafes, hanging out at the local drive-in restaurant, dicing in hotted-up cars and on motorbikes, partying and dating bad girls. An older friend, Chris Harding, had a hotted-up Ford Anglia with 'fat takkies' challenge stripes and the works. He was driving with me riding shotgun when we were passed by a hotted-up Mini. He put his foot down and we were catching the Mini when it suddenly turned right. Chris tried to follow but was going too fast to take the corner and the car rolled onto its side and into a ditch. Fortunately, neither of us was injured and there was not much damage to the car.

As a result of all the playing, I only passed one 'A' level subject (English with a B instead of the A of which I was capable). This meant I could not study law at the University of Rhodesia (then a College of the University of London) as I had planned. I was devastated having never really failed at anything before, but realised with the benefit of hindsight that it gave me the wake-up call that I needed. I managed to gain admission to the University of Natal in Durban, South Africa to do a BA (Bachelor of Arts) degree. Although I had a fairly enjoyable year in Durban, I worked really hard and did well in all my first year subjects. I also decided to rewrite 'A' level History, chose an earlier period which I found more interesting, studied on my own and achieved a B. I was then able to gain admission to the University of Rhodesia (UR) to study for a BL (Bachelor of Law) degree. Again, the pressure was on as, due to the demand for places, failing any subject in first year meant you could not continue with legal studies. Also, I was very aware of the fact that my mother (partly with money left by my late father) was funding my studies. Mum had moved from Salisbury to Rhodesia's second-biggest city, Bulawayo, so I stayed in residence. For my first couple of years at UR, I spent part of each vacation in Bulawayo. Despite working hard I thoroughly enjoyed my time at UR. During one of our University vacations, my friend, Brian Lambourne, and I travelled by train to Beira on the Mozambique coast. We chose the train because it was the cheapest way to get to Beira (where we camped) and a bit of an adventure. We were the only Whites on the train apart from the driver and conductor, who invited us to join them for drinks at various pubs along the way. No danger of missing the train as it only moved on when our drinks were finished!

My first car (*owned* by me alone) was the red Cortina my mother had bought new in London in 1963 and shipped out to Rhodesia. I had a great social life and fell head over heels for a girl called Pam Cleary. Her father had a friend who was a rich tobacco farmer and whom I remember for two good reasons. First, he owned a yellow Lamborghini (unfortunately I cannot remember the model), which he used to leave at the Cleary's house because it was too low to traverse the farm road. Mr Cleary took me for a drive in it; both of us were tall and I remember us being almost horizontal once in the car. Ever since, Lamborghini has been at the top of my most wanted list. The other reason I remember the farmer (although no longer his name) was tragic. Pam's parents often had lunch with the farmer at his farm and on one occasion she and I joined them. We had a good lunch with plenty of alcohol (including a dessert made by mixing ice cream and sherry). The farmer offered us a flip in his private plane, but we declined as we wanted to get back early for another function. Pam's parents left late in the afternoon by car and the farmer, as was apparently his custom, flew his plane above the main road and dipped one wing in farewell. On this occasion, however, the plane hit power lines and plunged to the ground and the farmer died on impact. Not long after that sad incident, Pam dumped me for someone else. Back in the days when we were still living with our parents or in University residences, cars were the best place to make-out with girls. I remember taking a date to the drive-in cinema (in the red Cortina,) to see the film "The Good, the Bad and the Ugly". With steamed up windows and other scenic attractions, all I remember about the movie is the theme music. We also used to frequent the 'shady parking' area at a local drive-in restaurant.

During my second year at UR, I met and started dating Karen Woodhouse. She was still at school studying for her GCE 'A' levels and was a well-known part-time model, having recently won an annual contest held by the local newspaper and become 'Rhodesia Herald Swinging Miss 1972.' Despite all the socialising, I managed to pass the BL with Upper Second Class Honours and the LL.B (Bachelor of Laws) with a mark of Distinction.

Chapter 4
MARRIAGE TO KAREN AND LIFE IN RHODESIA

In the early 1970s, life was still great in Rhodesia – if you were White. Ian Smith and his government had unilaterally declared independence from the British Government back in 1965. Despite economic sanctions imposed by most of the rest of the world, and an ever increasing level of attacks by Black 'freedom fighters'/'terrorists' (the chosen terminology depending on your, generally colour-bound, perspective), Karen and I had a privileged and pleasant lifestyle. Even as students we had access to servants – Black men who served as house boys – cleaning, cooking and doing all the other mundane household chores, usually with a happy smile, or as garden boys or waiters. It was around that time that I began to get worried about the sustainability of the political position and I wrote the following in my diary; it seemed clever at the time:

"The Europeans in Rhodesia are riding on the crest of a wave, and the only question is, when will the wave break? Surely it's better to hang back now while it's still deep enough to swim than to be smashed down onto the shore."

It took quite a few more years before the wave broke, and, in the meantime, Karen and I continued to enjoy our lifestyle. Although the civil war in Rhodesia was hotting-up, it was mainly a bush war which, at that stage, didn't impact much on those of us lucky enough to be in the cities and towns. However, I was liable to be called up for national military service and to become an unwilling participant. Many of my left-wing friends departed from Rhodesia illegally (attempting to avoid the call-up being a crime for which you could be arrested at the airport and jailed). My right-wing friends tended to accept, even welcome, the call to arms. I wasn't brave enough to 'take the gap', the so-called chicken run, but at the same time I was extremely reluctant to put my life on the line for a campaign which I did not support and, in any event, regarded as a lost cause. Fortunately, a colleague told me about the Directorate of Legal Services, which offered an opportunity for one or two lawyers each year to do their national service in relative safety and comfort. I applied, but was advised that there would be no more openings until the following year. So I managed to arrange a one-year post with the University of Rhodesia. I was taken on as a tutor and, due to the 'brain-drain' taking place in Rhodesia, I was promoted to lecturer almost immediately and ended up lecturing people who had been just one year behind me as students.

1976 was a significant year for me. I eventually embarked on my national service. I did four weeks of fairly tough basic training with the Air Force, was commissioned as an Air Sub-Lieutenant and started work as a legal officer with the Directorate of Legal Services (DLS.) DLS was a small, joint services unit. We dealt with such things as boards of inquiry:

investigations into vehicle accidents involving military personnel were the standard fare. There were also more interesting investigations into such things as alleged atrocities on the part of the Grey Scouts (mounted infantry) and alleged ivory trading on the part of the famed Selous Scouts, as well as courts martial. I became a fairly ineffectual prosecutor (having had no prior court experience) of regular and territorial soldiers charged with crimes like desertion/absence without leave, possession of dagga (marijuana,) insubordination, and theft.

On Saturday, 25 September, 1976, Karen and I were married in the City Presbyterian Church in Salisbury, Rhodesia. After the honeymoon, we were faced with the reality of married life. We rented and furnished a flat and went back to work. For me, that meant a continuation of national service. I guess I was one of the lucky few who actually enjoyed my military service, but who cannot lay claim to any heroic achievements (even looking back on things through the bottom of a beer glass!). For most of the time, I had an eight to five job in an office in central Salisbury in a building which also housed Air Force HQ (Headquarters) and Comops (Combined Operations) HQ. Apart from the fact that I wore the uniform of an Air Sub-Lieutenant in the Rhodesian Air Force (which my wife thought was sexy and compared me to the star of the movie "The Other Side of Midnight"), I could have been an ordinary lawyer going into the office every day with my briefcase.

As an Air Force officer, I had to do overnight duty in the Comops Ops Room from time to time. With my limited military training, I was out of my depth much of the time, noting sitreps (situation reports) and plotting them on maps for the 'real' (career) officers to examine in the morning. I hope I was not responsible for causing any aircraft accidents as civilian pilots telephoned the Ops Room to get permission to fly over certain areas. I had a fair idea what I was doing on that, but they would sometimes ask, "How's the weather at your loc (location)?" Now, I'm sitting in a room with no windows in the middle of a building at night and I have no idea what the weather is like, so my stock answer was "Weather fine!"

One night in the Ops Room all hell broke loose, with phones ringing and radio communications coming through. It turned out that our guys in the air were shooting at our guys on the ground. With much trepidation, I eventually used the red telephone to communicate with the top military brass and a number of senior ranking personnel came in and took over.

Karen got a job as a commercial artist and continued modelling part-time. She was Rhodesian Fashion Guild Model of the Year more than once and became something of a celebrity – doing fashion shows, dance shows and troop shows around the country.

Doing national service with the Air Force did give me the opportunity to spend some time in different aircraft. During basic training, we were taken up in an open-sided helicopter and, as the pilot banked it over for turns, I remember clutching onto the seat for fear of falling out; but of course centrifugal force keeps you in place. A squad of us had to jump out of the helicopter while it hovered above ground; I had the misfortune to be last to jump and the helicopter got higher off the ground as each airman alighted so the ground looked very far away by the time my turn came around. I also hitched a ride in a small military aircraft from Salisbury (now Harare) to Gwelo (now Gweru) and the pilot let me fly the plane while we were in the air. It was basically a matter of trying to keep it level and at the correct altitude, take-off and landing being the difficult parts of flying. While I was briefly based in Gwelo, a flying instructor took me up in his two-seater training aircraft, with trainees flying aeroplanes in formation beside and behind us. When you watch planes flying in formation, it looks smooth and you get no idea of how they (frighteningly) rise and fall independently of one another with wing tips appearing to almost touch. An opportunity I did not take up while based in Gwelo was to go parachuting. I met a parachute instructor at the officers' mess and he offered to train me to do a fixed line jump in a day. I chickened out and he went off to train others, returning to the mess in the evening with a broken arm – a strong wind having upset his landing!

The Director of Legal Services, the late Col John Reed, was a real character. He was a large man with a military bearing, a walrus moustache, pebble thick glasses, and a posh accent. He had been a District Commissioner and was fluent in various African languages, which resulted in some amusing incidents during courts martial when he corrected the court interpreter's translation of the accused's answer.

He was also a notorious womaniser and a heavy drinker. Friday night 'prayer meetings' were boozing sessions, which usually ended up with several of his subordinates carrying him to his car and one of us driving him home with another following. His staff car was a military green Peugeot 404 with a small flag on the bonnet. I once drove the Colonel from

Salisbury to Fort Victoria (now Masvingo) and return for a court-martial sitting in Fort Vic. He had me stop at every pub along the way and even though I moderated my drinking, I would have been way over the limit if stopped. Fortunately the police waved our military vehicle through their roadblocks.

It is said that you are not a true petrol head unless you have owned an Alfa Romeo. *My first and only Alfa* was a white Alfa Romeo 1750 which I bought second-hand around 1977. Like all Alfas, it was a fun car to drive but not very reliable. Marriage to Karen also gave me *my first sports car* (*shared* with her.) It was a red Triumph Spitfire (with a detachable hardtop) which had been hotted-up and had 'fat takkies' and a big air scoop on the bonnet. Karen had bought it second-hand before our marriage and I loved driving it. However, I did have an embarrassing incident using Karen's sports car. I went to a party without her as she had a modelling function, got far too drunk to drive myself home, but did so anyway, and had the only motor vehicle accident I have ever had which was my fault.

Fortunately it did not involve anyone else and all I did was turn too soon and drive the car into a deep ditch. I got some passing pedestrians to help me push the car out of the ditch and as we were doing this a police car came along. Fortunately for me, the policeman said that as long as I did not try to drive the car, he would leave it at that. In any event, the car was too damaged to drive. Karen's father, Dennis Woodhouse, like my father, was a motor mechanic. He had his own small vehicle workshop in Salisbury and had a tow truck. So, after walking to nearby shops to find a payphone, I had the embarrassing experience of phoning him in the early hours of the morning to come out and tow his daughter's car to his workshop and then drive me home to face my wife. Thankfully, he was a good bloke and we remained friends and my wife eventually forgave me.

My brother and I, with a couple of friends, bought a speed-boat with a Mercury 125 cc engine and we all got into boating and water-skiing. We had fun days and weekends at the local dam (Lake McIlwaine, the water supply dam for Salisbury) and long weekends and holidays at the magnificent Kariba Dam (then, the second-biggest man-made lake in the world). One of my fondest memories is of slalom skiing on Kariba in the late afternoon. Sunset in Africa can be majestic and nowhere more so than on Kariba – a golden orb in the distant sky, darkening through all the shades of orange and red, before eventually sinking over the horizon; creating on the water a magic pathway of the same changing colours, with splashes and sprays of pure silver. The water seemed to take on an oily, velvety texture and there seemed to be no sound but the swish of skis. The skyline was silhouetted, with clusters of dead tree trunks in front of a shoreline of all-black vegetation.

In those days, if you ventured out of the cities/towns by car, it was recommended that you should join a convoy. The convoy of civilian vehicles had a military escort, in the form of military vehicles at the front and back and roving alongside and, sometimes, an overhead helicopter. What scared me most about convoys was that, in addition to all the military weaponry, most of the civilian vehicles were bristling with rifles and handguns. I used to think that, in the event of an incident, the greatest danger would be getting caught in the crossfire between vehicles in the convoy.

On one trip to Kariba, we used the convoy, had a great holiday, and then set-off on the return journey. Karen, a girlfriend, and I in my Alfa, and a couple of friends in another car, arrived at the convoy collection point and were told that there would be a two-hour wait for the convoy. So we decided to go it alone – after all, we had a FN semi-automatic rifle (borrowed from the Air Force armoury) in my car, and something similar in the other car. The other car was travelling faster than my car and sped out of sight. Then my car got a puncture! We climbed out and I jokingly handed my rifle to one of my female passengers and said: "You stand guard while I change the wheel." Afterwards, we drove on to Salisbury, to hear later that the convoy we had avoided had been ambushed and that a mortar-bomb had taken out a bus. The Black bus driver and three young White girls were killed and sixteen other travellers in the convoy were injured. We had driven through the ambush site and changed a wheel not far beyond the killing zone, but they were waiting for the convoy. That sort of incident shows how little control you have over your own destiny.

During 1977, I completed the initial phase of my national service. Now was the time to do the travelling we hadn't had an opportunity to do before. It was now legal for me to leave the country, although it would still have been illegal for me not to return. So my wife and I set off with my brother and my good friend Ant Roberts on a voyage of discovery to Europe. Chris and I had visited Britain as children with our mother and grandmother, but Karen and Ant had never been out of Africa. At that time, Rhodesia was an international pariah – the group of us were able to get into Britain only because we all had

British passports through our fathers, except Karen who got in on a holiday visa as my wife.

We had, I now realise, a typical young overseas visitors' experience of Europe. First stop was London. We bought an old Bedford Campervan with a pop-up roof, in which we travelled up the east coast of Britain as far as Pitlochrie in the Scottish Highlands, then back down the west coast to London, with a side-trip to Northern Ireland, visiting friends and relatives along the way. A highlight for me was being driven in a friend of a friend's Porsche 911 to Silverstone to attend a race meeting.

A major problem with travelling anywhere from Rhodesia was that strict exchange control regulations and a poor exchange rate meant that you had access to a meagre amount of foreign currency. So, despite having led a fairly frugal existence in the UK, by this stage we had to get work there illegally or go home. I got a job packing Elizabeth Arden make-up into boxes at a factory outside London and Karen got a job selling the same make-up in a fancy salon on Bond Street. Working in that factory was an eye-opener, because for the first, and I hope only, time in my life, I had the opportunity to see things from the perspective of the working class, rather than from a position of privilege. An amusing memory which showcases the inequalities in life is of a young Irishman working at that factory. His life's ambition was to be a taxi driver, but he had already failed his driving test twice!

A *ménage a quatre* comprising a young married couple, plus two other men, living in the confines of a campervan in a campsite and commuting to work by train and bus was bound to fall apart, and did. But we were all marking time, saving cash to go across to the Continent. So we were surprised when Ant announced that he had had enough, moved into a flat in London for a while and then went home to Rhodesia. At this stage, Karen, Chris and I teamed up with Karen's pen-pal since childhood (an English girl none of us had met before this trip). We packed in our temporary jobs, packed up the campervan and headed to Dover via Plymouth, onto a ferry and over to France. A problem with the next stage of our trip was that my brother almost immediately developed an intense dislike of our new travelling companion. So if she was navigating and he was driving and she said "turn left here," he would turn right. This made for an extended tour of France, but we did manage to take in the sights of Paris (where we stayed in the overcrowded Bois de Boulogne campsite), as well as places like the French Alps, Monaco and St. Tropez. St. Tropez was a delight, especially for young Rhodesian men who had never been exposed to topless female bathers. At that time, Rhodesia had strict censorship and even Playboy magazine was banned. So, initially at least, to see real live topless girls was mind-blowing. On arrival at the campsite, I went into a toilet/change-room on the beach to change into my swimming costume, stopped off for a leak, turned around and dashed out of the door. I had been confronted by a pair of torpedoes attached to a shapely, tanned, female chassis, wearing the bottom half of a bikini. I assumed I was in the wrong loo, but a quick 360 degree look around the perimeter revealed that it was a single toilet block with a sign for "Hommes" at the end I had entered and a sign for "Femmes" at the other end. So Chris and I enjoyed a few days of bird watching, looking out in particular for the rarer, greater-titted varieties. Although I must say we also saw some horrible sights – whole families baring every shape and misshape under the sun - almost, but not quite, enough to put one off the whole concept.

From France, it was back to London to sell the campervan. We were sad to say goodbye to 'Benny Bedford' which had served us well as conveyance and home, and especially sad that we virtually had to give it away because its MOT (roadworthiness) certificate had expired. The four of us who had come over from Rhodesia together had originally planned that the next stage of our trip would be to fly to Germany in order to go to the Oktoberfest in Munich, then visit Amsterdam before flying home. Unfortunately, Ant had already gone home, Chris had a job interview to attend in Glasgow, and Karen and I had run out of money. So Chris went off on his own for the (unsuccessful) interview and then on to the Munich beer festival. Karen and I skipped Munich, but had a short visit to Amsterdam and experienced something of what it is like to be on the breadline. Before visiting Europe, we had bought Frommer's 'Guide to Europe on $10 a Day' (I think that was the dollar amount in that particular edition). At the back was a list of really cheap places to stay if you couldn't afford any of the recommended establishments. We ended up in a students' hotel in Amsterdam's notorious red-light district. The ground floor consisted of a bar, where we checked in and were offered drinks and drugs. Our room was up a long, circular, wooden staircase. It had a metal door with a padlock, which opened onto a double-bunk bed and that is literally all there was room for. But the worst of it was the communal showers. The lack of doors mattered not at all, because there were no lights. However, standing ankle-deep in cold, murky water, with a trickle of slightly less cold water running down your back, was quite a challenge.

Karen and I almost literally lived on bread and water as we had no money left. So we were pleased to board the flight home. Even South African Airways' food tasted great – to the extent that the lady sitting beside me noticed how I had scoffed down my meal with relish and offered me hers, which I accepted with gratitude, and scoffed down with equal pleasure.

Once back in Rhodesia, I started serving articles with a firm of attorneys. I was quickly "chucked in at the deep end". I had been a good law student, applying my mind to important, or at least interesting, issues like jurisprudence, delict (tort) and criminology. Now I was handling debt-collecting, matrimonial (divorce) matters and some other civil litigation. Instead of examining legal issues, I was dealing with legal procedures and bargaining. I had an uncomfortable feeling that I was not doing a good job for my clients. I was outside my areas of interest, expertise and experience and yet I was on my own – my principal, other superiors and even colleagues were too busy to assist. But the firm was still charging for the services, so it was the clients who were being screwed! And I was being assessed on how much business I was turning over for the practice. The blue-eyed boy in my firm at that time was handling an amazing number of files and earning huge fees for the firm, but I had the misfortune to take over a number of his cases and I soon realised that he was turning over quantity but not quality. Maybe, probably, that is the way to get ahead in legal practice, but I'm a great believer in the notion that quality will out.

Karen and I began to get the itch to travel again and somehow we hit upon the idea of my applying for a Rotary fellowship to do a postgraduate degree overseas. I duly applied and ended up as Rotary's second-choice candidate and was allocated my second-choice University. I got permission from my firm and from the High Court of Rhodesia to interrupt my articles and, early in 1979, Karen and I set off for Edmonton in Canada. I was enrolled to do an LL.M degree at the University of Alberta and we had arranged accommodation in the married student housing complex some way away from the campus. Beyond that, we were venturing into the unknown: from the heat and flames of Southern Africa in revolution, to the cold, ice and stability of Canada.

We had a wonderful time there. In fact, if I had been able to get a reasonable job offer, I think we would still be in Canada and I have often wondered how that would have changed our destinies. I had to put in a lot of work in order to complete the course work and dissertation for an LL.M (Master of Laws) degree in the one year sponsored by my Rotary fellowship. Karen was not allowed to work, but did end up augmenting our limited resources by doing baby-sitting, assisting with a research project on child development, and even doing paid housework – quite something for a young woman who had grown up in an environment where Black nannies did the baby-sitting and Black 'house boys' did the housework. So we both worked hard, but we also took full advantage of the opportunity to enjoy new experiences.

Neither of us had ever seen snow except in pictures and we were about to experience snow in abundance. I remember the first time it snowed. We were waiting at a bus-stop and it was getting dark although it was still early afternoon; soft, white things resembling tiny, crumpled pieces of paper, began to float down from the sky. This wasn't mist, rain or hail – suddenly we realised it was snow and we went out and tried to catch it, feel it, taste it. We held hands, kissed and danced around in the falling snow; we abandoned catching the bus to wherever we had been planning to go and went walking instead and nearly froze to death! After buying more appropriate clothing, we went on to enjoy the Canadian winter. No cabin-fever for us; we got out there and threw snowballs, made snowmen, and tried snow mobiles, tobogganing, ice-skating on a frozen lake, cross-country skiing, and downhill skiing. I can still picture the two of us in the late afternoon zigzagging down a reasonably gentle slope together. More independence and tranquillity than water-skiing, but with the same sense of danger and excitement. Silence, except for the crunch of skis biting into the crisp snow on the turns. Blue sky against the dazzling white of the snow. And the prospect of a warming drink and fireside chat at the bottom of the slope.

One of the features of our stay in Canada was our involvement with the International Students Association. This gave us the chance to meet students from all around the world and to visit some of Alberta's scenic attractions - including some stunning lakes and glaciers. In addition to the Canadians we met, we became friendly with people from England, India, South America, the Caribbean and Africa. A peculiar phenomenon, given our backgrounds, was how well we got on with people of colour, especially some Blacks from other parts of Africa. After initial unease on both sides, we found we had something in common: Africa. And one or two of them eventually told us that they appreciated the fact that we treated them in the same way as we treated everyone else. They had come to resent the White liberals who went out of their way to befriend and bed them, but who treated them as if they were circus sideshow freaks. Karen had been a good all-round sportsperson at school and had played netball, although only at school team level. Netball, however, is not a major sport in Canada and Karen managed to become the only White player in the Alberta netball team (who were mainly from the Caribbean.) And she even went on a team tour to British Columbia. This all resulted in our being invited to a couple of reggae parties where we were the only Whites; a turning of the tables, as back home in Rhodesia it had become fashionable to invite a few Blacks to White parties. I didn't have much time to play sport in Canada, but did try my hand at flag football (the US/Canadian equivalent of touch rugby) and racket ball (a second-rate version of squash!).

My academic supervisor was an elderly Indian gentleman by the name of Dr Khetarpal. He was a kind eccentric. He hated other Indians as a result of the fact that his young wife (imported from India) had long since run-off with an Indian graduate student. He fell for my young wife, invited us to his home on a number of occasions, made a play for Karen, told me how lucky I was, and warned me not to trust Indians! One of the benefits of having a Rotary fellowship was the appointment of a local Rotarian family as our counsellors. Mr & Mrs McNeil were a real boon. They were, to us, the epitome of retired, well off, Americans. Mrs McNeil had grey hair with a purple rinse and sucked boiled sweets. She was a pink lady – volunteers in pink overalls who helped out at the local hospital, a churchgoer and a general purveyor of apple-pie and motherhood.

After I got my LL.M, Karen and I flew to San Francisco. We were collected from the airport by my Aunt Maisie and Uncle Wally Reemelin in their red and white Cadillac convertible. They showed us around San Francisco, the Napa Valley, and their beautiful home in Meadow Vista, California. The Reemelins also took us to Lake Tahoe and to Reno, Nevada and we were in for more new experiences. In Reno, we stayed in a hotel suite that looked like a stage-set for the bedroom scene in a big-budget movie. I still have what I guess was a prophetic photo of Karen pretending to throw her wedding ring into a river – Reno being famous for quickie marriages and divorces.

All good things come to an end and in 1980 we came home to a country which was now called Zimbabwe-Rhodesia. This constituted a last-ditch attempt by the Rhodesian Front government under Ian Smith to preserve the *status quo* by purporting to accommodate Black liberation, through involving in government Bishop Abel Muzorewa and his party. What is interesting was the efficacy of the government propaganda machine – White Rhodesians had been treated like mushrooms: kept in the dark and fed on shit. They really believed that this was a workable solution, whereas we knew from our time overseas that the real power base lay with Robert Mugabe (reviled in Zimbabwe-Rhodesia as a Communist terrorist).

Karen and I moved into a rented cottage in the Salisbury suburb of Avondale and pretty much resumed our previous lifestyle. I went back to the law firm I had been with and discovered that I did not have to complete my articles and write the attorneys' admission exams. During the time I was away, the two components of the legal profession (attorneys and advocates) had been fused and all legal practitioners now had the same rights. As I had previously been admitted as an advocate, I was now able to gain admission as a legal practitioner without further ado. I did so, but I missed the academic environment and decided to go back to full-time law lecturing. The University of Zimbabwe was a very different institution from the University of Rhodesia. From a law department first year intake of about thirty, of whom about twenty-five were White, things had moved to an intake of about ninety, of whom about seventy were Black. A positive feature was an influx of academics from overseas. A negative was pressure to explain, and rectify, high failure rates and so to lower standards.

For the first time ever, one-man one-vote elections were held in the country. I was called-up to do roadblock duties. We were briefed by the police on what to do and, because I was a military officer, I was put in charge (at least in theory) of a joint services road-block unit. An amusing role-reversal was that my senior school geography teacher (a real disciplinarian whom we had all feared) was part of my unit and had to address me as "Sir." The unit included a number of prison services personnel who were none too bright and we had some comical exchanges on the radiotelephones: "Long-stop, Long-stop, this is Sunray, over."

(Silence)

"Long-stop, Long-stop, where are you?"

(Silence)

"Listen Piet, where the fuck are you?"

"I'm here in the ditch where you left me, where the hell else would I be?"

 "So why in shit's name didn't you answer?"

"Oh fuck, am I Long-stop?"

***

As Karen and I had predicted with the benefit of our overseas information, Mugabe swept into power and Zimbabwe was born. A nation which, despite all its initial promise, has been a big disappointment so far, especially for us (former) White liberals. Another one-man one-vote one-time, African State, which has come under the increasingly despotic rule of Robert Mugabe.

My brother got married during 1980 to Trish Johns and he and his wife and her two children, Gavin and Steven, left for Australia in 1981. That was a sad event for me and it highlighted the bombshell effect which had been happening in my country since I was at University. Whites were leaving in droves and heading for every corner of the earth – or, more accurately, any corner that would have them: mainly South Africa, Britain and Australia. Karen and I hung in and our first child, Adam Cant, was born on 29 September, 1981. I was there throughout the long labour and the birth and I remember wondering whether it would be fair ever to put my wife through that experience again. However, life went on, and, by the time we decided to move to South Africa, Karen was pregnant with our second child.

Chapter 5
MOVE TO SOUTH AFRICA AND DIVORCE

People often think that Whites left Zimbabwe for political reasons, especially those of us who moved to the last bastion of White minority rule: the Republic of South Africa. I'm sure that is true in many cases, but more pragmatic reasons applied in our case. Karen and I realised that we were getting nowhere – she was still a junior commercial artist and I was a law lecturer on a frozen salary, the Government having put a freeze on public sector salaries. I was keen to get a position as a legal adviser in commerce, but only a handful of Zimbabwean corporates were big enough to employ in-house legal staff. I wrote letters to all my contacts around the world saying I was looking for a job. The first thing that came up was an interview in Johannesburg, South Africa for the position of in-house legal adviser to a major financial services group, to replace an ex-Zimbabwean friend, Rich Barlow, who was moving on. I was offered the job and we took the big decision to make the move. At that time, there were severe restrictions on getting money out of Zimbabwe and I was advised that a quality sports car was a good way to do so. I looked into buying a second-hand E-Type Jaguar for the purpose, but unfortunately we could not afford it. So early in 1983, my pregnant wife, baby son and I, with all our luggage apart from some furniture and appliances sent by removal van, squeezed into our old Triumph Spitfire sports car. I will never forget that journey. Just out of Harare, it became clear that the car was over-loaded and was bottoming out on every bump. I considered turning back, but that would have been a real comedown after all the fond farewells, so I pressed on, driving slowly and taking bumps at an angle. The journey from Harare to Johannesburg is about 1200 kilometres in distance and, under normal circumstances, takes about thirteen hours by car. It took us nearly twice that time (excluding an overnight stop) and I guess we must have added a few hundred kilometres to the distance with our zigzagging over the bumps. We stopped-over at Beit Bridge and crossed the border into South Africa the next morning. I remember having a huge lump in my throat as I left the country of my birth. I knew that I would be back to visit, but that it was unlikely that I would ever live there again.

We initially viewed South Africa as a stepping-stone on the way to a new home, probably in Australia. "Two or three years," I said, "and then we'll either move on or even come back to Zims." After all, we were moving from the frying pan into the fire. From a country that had already undergone the heat and flames of transition to Black majority rule, to a country where that transition was widely expected to involve a major conflagration. And for good reason. The Rhodesian Front government of Ian Smith had tried for about fifteen years to keep the lid on a simmering pot of Black aspirations, until the pot boiled over. But the predominantly Afrikaans, National

Party government in South Africa had, since 1948, used barbed wire and brute force to clamp the lid on a boiling pot of Black demands. The policy of *apartheid* or separate development had led to racial conflict on an altogether different scale to what we had experienced in Rhodesia/Zimbabwe. Or so we thought. By some miracle, the eventual transition in South Africa was less fiery than in Zimbabwe – but I'm jumping the gun. Before I go back to the chronology of my diary, I must mention the irony of the failed plan to move on from South Africa. For years after my divorce, I believed that I no longer had the option of moving on because my sons were in South Africa; then they moved on!

Karen and I stayed with friends at Henley-on-Klip, then rented their new house, and eventually bought our own house, in Weltevreden Park, Johannesburg. The house we bought was our first own home and around that time I got *my first new car*, a silver Audi 100. This was also my first company car. It was a good, if unexciting, vehicle, but when I decided to sell it I had difficulty finding a buyer and vowed not to buy another Audi. Subsequently, Audis have of course become much more popular and I certainly wouldn't turn my nose up at an Audi R8! On 8 September, 1983, Karen gave birth to our second child, Christopher Cant.

For a few years, life was good. Karen and I worked and socialised in Johannesburg and holidayed in Durban and Zims with our sons. I took the opportunity to do a breakfast run on a motorbike. A friend of Karen's had a boyfriend who owned a motorbike shop. He lent me a 1200 cc Honda and we rode out to Hartbeespoort Dam with them. It was the most powerful bike I had ridden and, of course, I had to keep up with the other bikes – fun but terrifying at the same time. As my job as Group Legal Adviser at Sage Group involved advising on tax matters, I studied part-time at the University of the Witwatersrand and obtained a Higher Diploma in Tax Law. I also got involved in CLASA (Corporate Lawyers Association of South Africa), serving at various times as President and Vice-President and as editor of Incorporate magazine.

One of the companies in the Sage Group was Sandown Motors, a Mercedes-Benz dealership. Some work colleagues and I were having drinks with the dealer principal who was obviously a very good salesman as he persuaded three of us to buy new Mercs. So during 1985, I traded in the Audi for *my first Merc*, a silver 200 E. Another work colleague (who had a BMW) commented on my new car: "When you put your foot on the accelerator, the only thing that changes is the expression on your face." I admit that it was disappointingly sluggish and a couple of years later, I traded it in for *my second Merc*, a silver 230 E with somewhat better performance.

Unfortunately, things started to turn sour. In my relationship, where my wife was beginning to raise problems that I had not been aware of; and in the country, where the government had resorted to declaring a state of emergency because of ongoing strikes, sabotage and sanctions.

Karen and I agreed on a trial separation and on Sunday, 4 October, 1987, I moved out of the family home with a very heavy heart. I went to stay with a divorced friend, John Mehliss, who did law at the University of Rhodesia around the same time I did. I really missed my sons, but they stayed with us every second weekend, as did John's son, also called Chris, and we spent some quality time together: swimming, canoeing, hiking, braaing (barbecuing) and so on.

I also had a great visit to Zimbabwe with some friends. We flew to Victoria Falls and spent a night at the majestic old Vic Falls hotel. We had three days of kayaking on the Zambesi river above the falls; lots of fun and wonderful game viewing: lion, elephant, giraffe, crocodile, hippo, and all sorts of buck. Fortunately, none of the dangerous game came into our camps, which were on the banks of the Zambesi on stretchers under the stars. Our guide suggested we put the head-ends of our stretchers against trees and when asked "Why?" replied, "Well, if a lion attacks, wouldn't you rather he went for your feet than your head?" But don't get the wrong impression, this was camping in luxury. While we paddled down the river, the African staff went ahead in Land Rovers and set up camp: cold beers, good food, tables, chairs, even a tin bath and hot water for al fresco bathing. We spent a day white-water rafting in the Gorge below the falls. Really exciting stuff: inflatable boats, with an oarsman on a seat in the middle doing the steering and shouting instructions and seven passengers high-siding (diving onto the side of the boat which was about to hit a wave to avoid the wave flipping the boat), screaming and occasionally falling overboard.

The third leg of our trip was a walking safari and proved to be a disappointment, although amusing in retrospect. We travelled for three hours over bad dirt roads, packed into an old, slow Land Rover to reach our first camp in the Kazuma Depression on the border between Zimbabwe and Botswana. The next morning we went on a game-viewing drive and the guide took a wrong turning at a fork in the road, so began reversing and bang! Can you believe it? A three-vehicle pile-up involving what must have been the only three vehicles in a one hundred kilometre radius. It turned out that there was a Forestry Land Rover behind us and a National Parks Land Rover behind that – neither of which our driver had noticed, which was understandable given the cloud of dust thrown up by our vehicle. Anyway, the damage was minor and we pulled the vehicles apart and went on. We were dropped off in the middle of nowhere and we walked for most of the afternoon through hot, dry, thorn-scrub, which our guide assured us was teeming with game – of which, we saw little – or, more accurately, we saw a variety of distant, fleeing rumps. Until the second day when we nearly walked into a lioness with cubs, and then it was us running away! Our second camp was a minus-five-star establishment: not a patch of shade, nothing cold to drink, tiny tents, mopani flies and mosquitoes in droves. Up early for a nine-hour route march, carrying backpacks, which wouldn't have been quite so bad if I hadn't developed a really painful blister through wearing new walking shoes. We began to suspect that our guide had got lost, but he eventually led us to the pick-up point, where we commenced the long drive back to Victoria Falls. The old Land Rover was taking a hammering over the corrugations and I was just remarking on its resilience when the gear stick broke off in the driver's hand. Fortunately, we were stuck in fourth gear, so we were able to carry on and even chug up the hills by swapping into low-ratio. But then, there was a series of explosions, smoke poured out of the bonnet and we came to a grinding halt. By this time we had resigned ourselves to the fact that we would not be back in civilisation that night. A bloke in a station wagon came along and was persuaded (for a small fee) to take all of us and our kit to the Vic Falls airport.

My efforts to reconcile with Karen came to nothing and protracted divorce negotiations began. Saturday, 30th April, 1988 was another sad day for me. With the assistance of a friend who had a "bakkie" (a small truck), I collected my share of the household goods from what had been our final family home and transported them to my new townhouse. Once I realised that divorce was inevitable, I had hoped the ancillary matters could be sorted out amicably. Unfortunately, Karen brought in an aggressive attorney, which meant I needed an attorney and the bizarre phenomenon of bazaar-like bartering between the attorneys began. Eventually on Friday, 8 September, 1989, the Witwatersrand Local Division of the Supreme Court of South Africa granted me the divorce I had never wanted. I walked out of court with the mistaken notion that at least the hassles were over and I was free.

Chapter 6
LIFE IN SOUTH AFRICA AFTER DIVORCE

During my separation from Karen, I went out with several women and ended up in a relationship with Sherryl Myburgh, a secretary at Sage Group, where I was still working as legal adviser. After the divorce, I gradually settled into a different lifestyle. I lived on my own in a townhouse in Craighall Park, Johannesburg, but my sons stayed with me every second weekend and on other occasions including holidays away. Sherryl had her own townhouse, but often stayed over at my place and I often stayed with her on weekends when I did not have the boys with me. My townhouse was ideal for visits from my sons, as it had a swimming pool, tennis courts and a squash court and direct access onto a river trail where we did running and mountain biking together. I played squash, did aerobics and running, but I was dissatisfied with my life and drank to excess.

Following in my father's footsteps I have long had a hankering to fly. Not on long commercial flights which I dislike for two reasons: mild claustrophobia and having to fit my 6'3" frame into an economy class seat. I could not afford to train for a private pilot's licence, but hit on the idea of microlighting. I went for a paid flight with an instructor and loved it; like sitting pillion on a motorbike with wings! I was on the brink of signing up for a course and buying a microlight aircraft, but was put off by a couple of things: first, that my life insurance premiums would have soared and second, that it was an expensive and selfish sport in that I could never have taken more than one passenger and I was sure my ex-wife would not allow me to take my sons. So, like my dad, flying is an ambition I have not achieved.

My brother, his wife and their children, Emma and Matthew, came out to South Africa during 1988 and all of them, plus my two sons and I, squeezed into my Mercedes 230E to travel to Durban and then to Zimbabwe, where we spent time in Harare and Kariba. At Kariba, we had a frightening experience on a friend's small cabin cruiser. With four adults and four small children on board, we were out near the middle of the Dam when one of the two motors packed up; we were then chugging slowly back to Caribbea Bay when a storm struck bringing huge waves. Our friend, Bimbo Westland, asked my brother to take the helm as Chris had experience of boating on the sea. He then radioed the Dam's control tower and requested assistance, but was told they had no available rescue boat! Fortunately, we were able to complete the slow and perilous journey on our own, but never have I felt more relieved to get back on dry land. Sherryl and I spent Christmas 1989 and New Year 1990 in Cape Town and then drove up the garden route to Plettenberg Bay. I did another canoeing expedition with friends during 1990, this time on the Orange River in South Africa.

During 1990, I decided that I wanted a sportier car than the Merc 230E. The Merc dealership from which I had bought the car was also a Honda dealership and the dealer principal showed me various other Mercs and Hondas; I ended up buying *my first sports car* (*owned* by me alone), a silver (again!) Honda Prelude. I still think that particular model Prelude (which was apparently designed for the US market) was the best looking car Honda has produced. It also cornered like a go-kart, but I came to think of it as a sheep in wolf's clothing because its acceleration did not match up to its looks.

Unfortunately, my notion that the divorce would be the end of the hassles couldn't have been further from the mark. Now began ongoing and often acrimonious correspondence between Karen and me regarding our sons: my contributions, access arrangements, where they should go to school and so on.

While I was preoccupied with the developments in my personal life, there were many significant political developments in South Africa. PW Botha ("die groot krokodil," the finger-wagging Afrikaner, who couldn't bring himself to cross the Rubicon) was succeeded by FW de Klerk (the amiable-looking, chain-smoking Afrikaner, who did cross the Rubicon). Nelson Mandela ("Madiba," the Black activist who went on to become the 'father of the nation' in the new South Africa and one of the most famous politicians of all time) was released from jail. The ban on the African National Congress (ANC, the enemy of the White nationalists during the years of the total onslaught) was lifted, and the state of emergency (modern-day parlance for martial law) was lifted. Constitutional negotiations were underway, but there was widespread conflict in the country, as well as in my relationships!

From late November, 1993, there was a noticeable change in the style and content of Karen's letters. I only realised later that they were now being written by the new man in her life, Derek Smith. I had vaguely hoped that if Karen found another man, she would get off my back. But it transpired that with the advent of this man in her life, things went from bad to worse and eventually to worse still. The correspondence became increasingly acrimonious. And I have to confess that I was reminded often of the joke to the effect that, for them, a battle of wits was unarmed combat.

Karen married Derek in February 1994. South Africa's first one-person-one-vote elections also took place during 1994 and were won by Nelson Mandela's African National Congress. Thus began a brand-new era for South Africa, but nothing so exciting for me. I had to deal with an application for increased maintenance for my sons and then a visit from the Sheriff of Randburg to attach property of mine in respect of arrears maintenance and legal costs. As I was able to establish that there were no grounds for an increase in maintenance and no arrears owed, these matters fell away, but cost me in time, money and stress. Continued disputes regarding maintenance, provision of clothing for the boys during their visits with me and access arrangements resulted in further costs and stress.

However, there had been some highlights. On 28th March. 1991, I wrote the following:

> *"In the absence of any available person with whom I feel like sharing my thoughts at this moment, I decided to try to record them.*

The situation I am in, given my usual fairly humdrum existence is, to say the least, surprising. I still have to pinch myself to check that it is really happening and not a dream. After years of complaining that my job involves no travel at all, it is incredible to think that in the past five weeks, I have been to London twice, Madrid once, and I have spent most of my time on the Costa del Sol in Spain, all on business. And I have taken the opportunity to visit many of the tourist attractions of Andalusia.

Right now my surroundings are, at least on the face of it, idyllic. It is early evening, still daylight and fairly balmy. I'm sitting on the porch of a luxury apartment in an up-market resort development (Miraflores) on the Costa del Sol between Fuengirola and Marbella. I am looking out over the Mediterranean, with Gibraltar and even the hills of North Africa just visible on the horizon. Although not right on the beach, I'm close enough to hear the roar of the sea as it pounds in over the rocks. I have a San Miguel lager (not bad) at one hand and a dish of Spanish olives (superb) at the other. I earlier had a few slices of Serrano ham (Spanish biltong/jerky) as a snack and I am going to heat up a seafood pizza and open a bottle of Spanish red wine (lousy) for dinner.

Henri Staub (the expatriate South African MD of the resort development company co-owned by my employer company and the South African Breweries) had invited us to go through to Malaga with him and his family to watch the Easter festivities. Dave Langham (a colleague from South Africa who presently has the apartment above mine at Miraflores) and I decided to have a quiet evening on our own (and separately) for a change. As well as imposing on the hospitality of Henri and his wife from time to time, Dave and I have dined out fairly frequently whilst we have been here. And we have experienced the whole range of quality and service. From the best paella I've ever had (in the quaint mountain village of Mijas) and the best seafood gumbo I've ever had (in a small 'English' pub near here), to a paella that made us both ill (at the beach restaurant just below our apartments) and some very questionable fish (at a fancy restaurant in the up-market coastal resort of Puerto Banus. The service in Spanish restaurants seems to range from poor to non-existent.

That is where the mixed feelings about this place begin to come in. Maybe Dave and I are biased because of the circumstances in which we are seeing it: on business, before the summer season, and in a bad year for European tourism. But I can honestly say that I would rather be on holiday (or business) in Durban or Cape Town, South Africa. Although this place has its attractions, it is over-developed and yet (out of season) empty, generally grubby, and full of low-class Spaniards and expat Brits who offer, at best, mediocre service. Although there is evidently wealth around, one gets the impression that it is mainly "black" money from drug dealing and other crime. And the people lack refinement. Wealthy Arabs and Brits with Rolls-Royce convertibles in bright, metallic colours; smooth operators from around the world from whom I'd be reluctant to buy a second-hand car. Scruffy European tourists; low-class Poms, who live here and run pubs offering 'real British fish & chips,' and the even lower-class Poms, who come out on package trips to get drunk and savour their own cuisine; and, of course, the Spaniards, who display a lot of pride and little reason for it.

There are places of great natural beauty – sunset right here can be unbelievable – but don't look too closely as the beaches are polluted and most things look better from afar. There are picturesque village squares with slums just a few streets away, impressive developments cheek by jowl with dreadful high-rises and empty shopping centres. A general impression of over-development and poor administration. Getting used to driving on the wrong (right) side of the road is bad enough, but right-angle entrances onto freeways, narrow roads, potholes and broken verges make it worse. I also have mixed feelings about business travel in general and this episode in particular. On the one hand, I was delighted to have the opportunity. I have enjoyed various aspects and I have learned some useful lessons; in particular about handling negotiations involving people in different countries (in this case Spain, Britain and South Africa).

On the other hand, I have experienced a lot of frustration in the work context and some boredom and loneliness. I've come to the realisation that many business people and lawyers worldwide are ineffectual or worse. Getting instructions from my superiors in South Africa on urgent matters has been particularly frustrating.

One other aspect, before I close off and watch television. Since I've been here, I have missed Sherryl and

I have realised that she means a lot more to me than I had thought before I left. I miss her company to a greater extent than I had anticipated: good company as they may be, other people like Dave just don't come up to scratch when it comes to things like sightseeing and dinners out. My immediate thinking is to ask her to marry me not long after I get back to South Africa: let's see."

***

After my return to South Africa, Sherryl and I continued to go out together, but we had some problems and she did not want to get married to me. I turned forty on 28 November, 1991 and Sherryl arranged a fun birthday party for me. She hired an open-top, double-decker bus on which we partied while driving around Joburg's northern suburbs. After that, the party continued in a marquee in a friend's garden. In January, 1992, I became Group Company Secretary at Sage and now headed two small departments, Legal and Company Secretarial (to which Compliance was later added).

Early in 1992, I did a great road trip to Zimbabwe with eight other guys from South Africa, (two of us being ex-Zimbabweans). First stop was Hwange Game Reserve which then still had a magnificent array of wildlife including large herds of Sable Antelope. Then on to the incredible Victoria Falls – aptly named Mosi-oa-Tunya (the smoke that thunders) by the local people. You need to wear a raincoat to walk through the 'rain forest' which is continually drenched by spray from the water thundering over the falls. We stayed at the old colonial style Victoria Falls Hotel, which at that time, had a well-known doorman wearing a red coat and black top hat both covered in medals. We visited the Elephant Hills Hotel (to take in the view from the deck and drink Zambesi lager), the Southern Sun Hotel (to gamble and drink Zambesi lager) and the Rainbow Hotel (to listen to the Marimba band and drink Zambesi lager).

We then packed plenty of cases of Zambesi lager into three Land Rovers towing trailers with canoes on racks and were driven to a place deep in the bush on the Zambesi River above the falls. On that drive we saw a pride of lion sleeping right next to the road, elephant, giraffe and various species of antelope. On the first night, our guide Paul Connolly (who owned the safari company but did the guiding on this occasion as two of us had been at University with him) said that perhaps the next night we would not drink quite so much after a full day canoeing on the river – but he was wrong! We spent three happy days canoeing on the river in Indian style two-man canoes, much of it on flat water, but with some exciting stretches of white water. I was in a canoe with my friend, John Mehliss, and on one occasion when our canoe turned over in a rapid, he got caught up in the splash cover and nearly drowned. Thereafter, as we approached each rapid, you could hear John ripping open the splash cover, so he became known for the rest of the trip as 'Velcro Mehliss.' It appears that wild animals do not expect danger to approach from the water so the game viewing from the boats was incredible. I have video footage I filmed from the canoe of a herd of elephant helping each other to climb up a steep bank out of the water just a few yards away from us. The riverbanks were teeming with crocodiles, hippo and various other game; the main danger to the boats being hippo, but apparently they are territorial and our guide knew which areas to avoid, although we still had some occasions when a hippo popped up out of the water near our canoes and we suddenly became world beating paddlers flying across the water out of harm's way. We spent the nights drinking, eating and talking and then sleeping, all out in the open under a magnificent canopy of stars that you only see when you are in the bush.

We took the canoes out of the water just above the falls and went back to the hotel. The next day was spent white-water rafting in the Kariba gorge below the falls. In a state of beer induced bravado the night before, half of our party (including me) decided to go on a paddle boat, a rubber duck on which you each have a paddle and paddle yourselves with assistance from a guide at the back also with a paddle. The others chose an oar boat, a rubber duck on which the guide steers and paddles the boat with a long oar from a seat in the middle. So we called ourselves 'the A team' and the others 'the jelly babies.' It is amusing to watch the professional video of 'the A team' going into the rapids to see who dives into the boat to avoid falling off and who was brave enough to keep paddling until just before the wave hit the boat. Of course, all of us spent time in the water, but one of the jelly babies had the worst experience as he fell out of the boat at the first of a succession of three rapids so was a free swimmer throughout.

We drove from Victoria Falls to Kazungula at the West end of Kariba dam and took the overnight car ferry from there along the length of the dam to Kariba. Great fun, sitting out on the deck all night, playing liar dice and cards and drinking more Zambesi lager. Then we had a few days on a houseboat on Kariba dam. The captain's name was Passmore and, as the bridge from which he steered the boat was next to the fridge, he soon became known as 'Passmore beer'. We had a fun time, fishing for Tiger fish and bream from the tender boat, diving from the top of the boat into the dam and swimming quickly to the stairs (in case of crocs, although they supposedly stay near the shore), visiting hotels on some islands and generally enjoying ourselves. From Kariba, we drove to the fascinating Zimbabwe Ruins (or Great Zimbabwe Monuments as they are now called) via Harare and then back to Joburg.

I got into running and, in 1992, succeeded in running the Two Oceans Marathon (fifty-six kilometres) in Cape Town within the six hour time limit. In the same year, I ran the Comrades Marathon (about ninety kilometres from Durban to Pietermaritzburg) in a little less than the eleven hour cut-off time. And the next year, I did the Comrades 'down' run (Pietermaritzburg to Durban) slightly faster.

During 1992, Sherryl and I made the first of several trips to Zimbabwe with a group of friends in two VW Kombis, which eventually took in all of the main attractions including Victoria Falls, Kariba, Inyanga, Vumba, Zimbabwe Ruins, Harare and Bulawayo. Over the years, we, mainly with family and friends, visited most of South Africa's main attractions, including the Kruger and Pilansberg game reserves, the Drakensberg Mountains, the Natal Midlands, the Lowveld, Namaqualand, the Cape Winelands and most coastal resorts and towns on the Western Cape, Eastern Cape, and Natal Coasts. We have also made a few visits to neighbouring Mozambique.

Early in 1993, I had the opportunity to go to Singapore for a convention with FPS Insurance Brokers (a company in the

Sage Group), and I went on to visit my brother and his family in Perth, Western Australia. I ran the London Marathon in April 1994 with three friends, and, despite stopping for photos and beers, we managed to complete the distance in four hours, forty-four minutes, and forty-four seconds.

I took my sons and Sherryl to Perth (via Singapore) to visit my brother and his family over the Christmas 1995 and New Year period and we had a wonderful time. We drove in a hired Land Cruiser to Monkey Mia to swim with the dolphins, but for the first time in ages the dolphins chose not to come inshore. On the way back to Perth, we drove along the beach and at one point stopped for a swim in the sea. Sherryl, understandably, panicked when she saw a fin coming towards her, which she assumed to be a shark and she shouted for all of us to get out of the water. Imagine our disappointment when it turned out that 'Jaws' was a dolphin with a calf which had come in to swim with us!

My mother and stepfather, George Harwood, were also in Perth and it was good to have the opportunity to discuss with my family my ongoing problems with the Smiths. I was dreaming and scheming about how I could just stay in Australia with Sherryl and the boys and the rest of my family, and never go back to the reality of my normal existence. No such luck however, and back we came to Johannesburg early in 1996.

Chapter 7
"LOSS" OF MY SONS AND OTHER HASSLES

Towards the end of October 1996, I received, out of the blue, the letter all non-custodian parents dread. Karen and Derek advised of their intention to emigrate from South Africa to the USA and requested my agreement to their taking my sons with them. After much soul-searching, discussion with family and friends and correspondence, I agreed on the basis that I would pay slightly reduced maintenance (calculated in SA Rands) and the savings would contribute towards the cost of my bringing the boys to South Africa for an annual holiday.

Around this time, Sherryl, my girlfriend for most of the nine years since my separation from Karen, had terminated our relationship. My brother and I had been planning a get-together in Britain, including a visit with our mother, since before I received the dreaded letter about the proposed removal of my sons from South Africa and before Sherryl ended our relationship. I did consider cancelling my trip to be with the boys right up until their departure for the USA, but I decided that that would be even harder to handle. As it was, the parting was the biggest wrench I have experienced. And that's saying something. I had gone through the deaths of my father and my grandmother, the departures for other countries of my brother and my mother, my own move from the land of my birth, and of course, my divorce.

I will never forget the last time I saw my sons before their move to the USA. It was a Monday morning. Adam had a bout of gastric flu which had put paid to most of my plans for our last weekend together and I dropped him off at his mother's house to go back to bed. A final quick squeeze (as a cool fifteen-year-old he was no longer into kissing his father) and I watched him walk off up the driveway. I had a big lump in my throat but I knew he would be okay. Then I dropped off Chris, on a street corner, to wait for his lift to school. He was a bit younger and more demonstrative so we were able to have a kiss and cuddle. Imprinted indelibly on my mind is the picture of Chris, standing on that street corner in his school uniform, sobbing and waving as I drove away. I was also waving and sobbing. Clearly, I'm not a cowboy!

Going off on holiday in Britain with the rest of my family was the best thing I could have done at that time. I hate to think how I would have coped at home on my own. As it was, I didn't cope all that well on holiday. I was okay as long as I shut off my mind to the "loss" of my sons. I couldn't even bring myself to talk about the situation to my brother or my mother. Isn't it ridiculous that my muscular Christian, stiff upper-lip background prevented me from revealing my feelings even to my own family? When the topic came up, instead of letting off steam, I fought back the tears, swallowed the lump in my throat and changed the subject. A problem for me in bottling up my emotions is that they seem to find their release through the bottle; so I get maudlin or, like the cork out of a champagne bottle, I explode into space and then fall back to earth. Anyway, most of the holiday was fun, but eventually I had to face the reality of being home and by myself.

But there were some consolations. Karen and Derek were out of my hair. The boys were getting a great opportunity to settle in the USA which I could not have given them. I could be with them for their long vacation every year and we had made exciting plans: South Africa in 1998, the US in 1999 and Australia in 2000. And, of course, we could maintain regular contact through e-mail in particular, and also through phone and even snail-mail.

Things got off to a reasonable start. I re-established a limited sort of relationship with Sherryl. I made my agreed monthly contributions towards the maintenance and education of my sons. And, although the amount of communication from their side was disappointing, we were in contact and we did manage to plan for their visit to South Africa in mid-1998.

Early in 1998, Sherryl and I, with a large group of friends, had a fun holiday in Turkey – taking in the attractions of Istanbul and Marmeris and spending a few days sailing on a Gulette. The girls had secretly taken belly-dancing lessons and treated the men to a show on the Gulette and as a guest act at a resort in Marmeris.

Around this time, I bought *my first BMW*, a white (for a change) 328i convertible; a really enjoyable vehicle.

The visit from Adam and Chris was wonderful. In the year since I had last seen them, Adam had gone from boy to man, but it didn't take long to re-establish a rapport and to find that he had developed into a fine young man. And Chris was still the same great guy it had broken my heart to bid farewell. They were with me for a couple of activity-packed months, which I can recapture by watching the video which I filmed and they edited. "Back to Africa" they called it and it would make a good tourism advert for southern Africa.

I live and work in Johannesburg so that was our base, and we took in some of the attractions of Egoli (the city of gold) and its environs. The three of us then drove down to Umhlanga Rocks on the Natal coast near Durban and spent a week in a timeshare hotel doing all the seaside things together – swimming, body-surfing, bird (non-feathered variety) watching, jogging, eating seafood, going to the aquarium and the dolphin show. Back to Joburg and my mother and stepfather (who were lucky enough to live in England for half the year and in Australia for the other half) joined us for a trip to Mpumalanga (formerly known as the Eastern Transvaal). We stayed in another timeshare resort, this time next to a lake. A three-generation get-together can be difficult, but this one worked: with shared activities like walking, (feathered) bird-watching, barbecuing and sight-seeing (incredible mountain-views, waterfalls, gorges, old mining villages); and the boys doing their own thing – making friends, rowing, playing tennis and taking part in organised games. We also spent a day in the world-renowned Kruger National Park where we saw a fantastic array of wild animal and bird life, including elephant, buffalo, giraffe, zebra, hippo, crocodile, and a variety of antelope, as well as my favourite bird: the lilac-breasted roller (common in the Kruger Park, but with striking multi-coloured glossy plumage).

Next stop was the little town of Rhodes in the Northern Cape, which is host each winter to a mountain running race over a distance of fifty-two kilometres under freezing conditions. I've done the race once. But Sherryl and some of her friends used to run the race every year and it is a very festive event, with the runners and supporters taking over the village and its two pubs for the weekend. A short but treacherous drive in a 4 x 4 takes you from Rhodes to Tiffendel, which is the only snow-ski resort in South Africa. So, while my friends were running the ultra-marathon, my sons and I were snow skiing in Africa.

The last port-of-call was Harare in Zimbabwe. Sherryl, my sons and I drove up in my car (no mean feat fitting four adults with luggage into a BMW 328i convertible). We dropped the boys with their maternal grandparents who had a farm just outside Harare and Sherryl and I stayed with friends in Harare. We also spent a couple of days at a private game reserve where we rode on elephants, played with a lion cub, canoed on the river and saw a wide variety of game.

It was all over too soon and it was another real wrench to see my sons off again. Unfortunately, however, things were destined to get worse. It started with an innocuous-sounding letter from Derek dated 16 July, 1998, asking for my thoughts regarding meeting the costs of Adam's tertiary education.

I replied to the effect that my stance was unchanged: although I was not able, willing, nor obliged, to have their move to the US result in an increase in the amount of my contributions (in Rand terms), I was prepared to pay the full amount I would have had to pay if the boys had been here in South Africa. In the course of further correspondence, I gave an indication of that Rand amount, based on information I had obtained from local universities and from friends with children at universities in South Africa. Further correspondence with Derek, then his attorney, then Adam, and then Karen, ensued, but achieved nothing.

I had problems trying to arrange a get-together with my sons during 1999. The original plan had been for me to visit them in the US, but apparent lack of interest on their part caused me to offer them the alternative of coming back to South Africa for their long mid-year holiday. Then my brother suggested a family reunion and week-long party in Perth, Australia, to celebrate the new millennium so I offered my sons the opportunity of joining me in Australia at year-end as another possibility for our 1999 get-together. Adam chose not to take up any of those offers but Chris decided to come out to South Africa on his own in July instead. His last-minute decision cost me a lot of extra money but our holiday together was worth it.

Sherryl's mother and stepfather had retired and lived in a lovely seaside home in the quiet coastal town of East London, South Africa. Sherryl stayed at the house and Chris and I stayed at a nearby hotel for a fun week during Chris' visit. Then he and I had another enjoyable week at Umhlanga Rocks on the Natal coast.

In December, 1999, Sherryl and I travelled to Australia. First stop was Perth to visit my brother and his family. We had a good time, but I overdid the drinking to the extent that Sherryl threatened to go home to South Africa and leave me to holiday on my own. I wound my neck in and I think I behaved reasonably well thereafter. Together with an ex-South African couple who had just moved to Australia, we took the ferry from Perth to Rottnest Island. We were amused by the fact that, being used to relatively lax safety standards in South Africa, they had brought their own lifejackets for their children – onto a ferry equipped with every imaginable safety device which were demonstrated to us in aircraft fashion. By contrast, I was reminded of an occasion when Sherryl and I did a sunset cruise from Durban harbour on an old, small boat packed with people out for a party; with music blaring and no noticeable safety devices except for a few lifejackets. We ventured out into open sea despite the Captain's warning that it would be rough out there! We spent Christmas in Perth and New Year at Smith's Beach (a resort down-south of Perth.) Then we flew to Sydney and met up with friends and family and had a wonderful time enjoying all the sights and experiences. The harbour with the famous opera house and bridge; a trip on a replica of the Bounty; visits to Manly, Ku-ring-gai Chase National Park, Bondi Beach, and the new Olympic stadium.

From Sydney to Cairns. There we experienced snorkelling on the Barrier Reef, which has to be one of life's greatest experiences: on a par, for me, with water-skiing on Kariba Dam, Zimbabwe at sunset; snow skiing at Jasper, Canada; and white-water rafting in the Zambesi gorge, Zimbabwe. The utter tranquillity of floating face-down in balmy water, with no sound except your own breathing; turning and moving with the slightest of body movements; feeling as if you are part of the underwater world. And what a world! Coral like a spectacular garden, inhabited by fish of every imaginable colour, pattern and shape. We also viewed the underwater world from the comparatively claustrophobic confines of a glass-bottomed boat.

After Cairns, we flew to Brisbane and met up with a former work and running colleague from South Africa, Alan Mitrovich. Lots of fun and then back to Johannesburg via Sydney.

A few days after getting back to my office in Johannesburg following the trip to Australia, I was told that the Sheriff of the High Court was at the reception desk. I assumed it was a company matter and asked that he be brought to my office. I was then served with a notice of motion, claiming a huge increase in maintenance for my sons based on US costs (contrary to everything that had been agreed). The amount claimed was over six-thousand Rand per month more than my total net monthly income (before expenses)!

Yet again, I was thrust into the clutches of the legal system. Despite my previous experiences at the hands of the legal profession, I believed that I had no choice but to obtain top-level legal representation. After all, this was a High Court application and if through some miscarriage of justice it succeeded, I would be financially crippled. I toyed with the idea of using a well-known matrimonial specialist with a reputation as a no-holds-barred fighter, but was put off by his reputation for no-holds-barred charging. In discussion with a couple of attorney friends in commercial practise, I was given the name of another matrimonial specialist, but it turned out that she only handled divorces, not post-divorce maintenance matters. She recommended another female attorney (solicitor), whom I ended up using and who, rather confusingly, had the same name as my ex-wife. As it was a High Court matter, this

Karen brought in a female advocate (barrister) who also specialised in matrimonial matters.

I spent hours in consultation with my lawyers, and many more hours on my own, going through the founding affidavit and annexures, as well as my own files of correspondence with my ex-wife and preparing an answering affidavit with annexures. I wanted to take a hard-line, totally opposing the application and counter-claiming for custody/repatriation of my sons on the basis that it was clear that my ex-wife was unable and/or unwilling to comply with her agreed obligations. However, I was persuaded actually to tender an increased amount of maintenance and not to try to counter-claim for the boys to be returned to South Africa.

It seems that troubles in my personal affairs often have coincided with troubles in the country. This time there were serious problems in the land of my birth (Zimbabwe), which were spilling over into my adopted homeland (South Africa). What was happening in Zimbabwe was unbelievable. I had felt for a long time things in that country would never get as bad as in South Africa because there had never been the same levels of racial repression and hostility. As recently as a few years before, I had even considered the possibility of going back there if the situation here became intolerable. Who would believe that twenty years after independence and Black majority rule, Zimbabwe's economic plight (by then much worse than it was at independence) was being blamed on the Whites and on Britain? In fact, on anyone other than the real culprit: the increasingly irrational and despotic President Robert Mugabe – who seemed to be determined to stay in power at all costs? That White farms were being violently invaded by so-called war veterans? And that White farmers and their families, as well as Black farm-workers and members of the opposition party, were being murdered, raped and beaten, without intervention by the international community, or even condemnation by then South African President Thabo Mbeki?

The Zimbabwe crisis contributed to the South African Rand falling to an all-time low against the US Dollar and some other overseas currencies, as well as to an outflow from South Africa of investments from offshore. It also led me (and many others) to again question the future of Whites in Africa. Violent crime, majority repression of the "pale male" through affirmative action and apparently unending blaming of colonisation and apartheid for all problems were bad enough; and were already driving out younger, skilled Whites in droves. Now, we had yet another example of democracy and law and order going out of the window. If White farms in Zimbabwe could be invaded to redress perceived inequalities in land distribution, why shouldn't the same happen in South Africa? And if farms could be invaded on that basis, why not businesses and even homes? Free and fair elections or one-person one-vote one-time?

A friend with whom I was discussing this issue commented: "Although you obviously miss your sons badly, you must be glad that they are out of Africa."

"Ja, well, no, fine," was my typically South African response. Translated into better English, a typical lawyer's response: "Yes and no."

If it was reasonably feasible for them to get their tertiary education in the US and to have the option to live there, that had to be first prize. But the significant fall in the Rand against the Dollar highlighted my inability to make a meaningful contribution in Dollar terms. And, if the only way they could stay there would have left them or me penniless, then they should have come back to South Africa. And, who knows, this country just might have turned out to be the land of opportunity that my parents thought Rhodesia would be when they immigrated there more than half a century ago!

One thing is strikingly clear to me: lawyers in private practice, who set their own fees irrespective of outcomes and who therefore have a pecuniary interest in escalating and protracting matters, should have no part in the resolution of matrimonial disputes.

Clear evidence of this notion is to be found in what went on to happen in the High Court claim against me for a ridiculous increase in the maintenance payable for my sons. My ex-wife, through her lawyers, had instituted the claim. I, through my lawyers, filed an answering affidavit and counter-claim (relating mainly to the calculation of the maintenance in SA Rands rather than US Dollars), but nevertheless tendered an increased amount of maintenance. Thereafter, we even granted a couple of extensions for their response. But nothing further was heard from my ex-wife or her attorney.

As a result, my attorney threatened and then proceeded, to set the case down for hearing. Nobody from the other side showed up for the hearing and my lawyers could simply have asked for the application to be dismissed with costs. They, however, without consulting me, proceeded with the counter-claim/tender. This had the beneficial effect of obtaining a court order clearly stipulating that the maintenance would always be calculated on a SA Rand cost basis. But it also had the effect of significantly increasing the amount of maintenance payable by me: something I had been prepared to agree to in the face of a claim for a huge US Dollar-based increase, but would not necessarily otherwise have gone along with.

Chris came out to South Africa again in July, 2000 and, after his visit, I made the following entry in my diary:

> *"16 July, 2000*
>
> *Yesterday, I took my younger son to the airport and saw him off to the US after another wonderful holiday together. Again, the final hug brought a lump to my throat and tears to my eyes. But I was also at the airport to meet a friend who had flown in from Australia. So I choked back my emotions and even managed to go out for an enjoyable dinner with my friend.*
>
> *Today, however, I have been on my own and I simply couldn't bottle it up any longer. I sobbed uncontrollably for a while and hoped the neighbours couldn't hear me. Knowing that what I am feeling is pure self-pity (because the boys themselves are fine) doesn't make it any easier. My tears were tears of frustration rather than tears of sorrow. I'm really happy when I'm with my sons so why should I have (at best) only three or four weeks out of each year with them? In theory, they're supposed to be with me for at least two-thirds of their long vacations (one or two months) but that isn't practicable for me in terms of leave time and costs and isn't fair for them in terms of having a life in the US: vacation jobs, summer holidays, fun with friends. It seems clear that they will never come back to*

this country to live. So short of moving elsewhere myself (which I am contemplating, but Australia not US), it seems there is nothing I can do to improve the situation. And moving could make it even worse if I could no longer afford to pay for the get-togethers with my sons."

After many hassles in making arrangements, Adam came to South Africa in January, 2001 and, afterwards, I made the following diary entry:

"29 January, 2001

Yet another sad farewell. Last Thursday evening, I took my elder son to the airport and saw him off – back to the States and out of my life for at least another year. I wish I could say that the lump in my throat gets smaller each time, but it doesn't. I choke trying to say goodbye and the pain in my throat matches the hurt in my heart. For days afterwards I burst into tears and sobs of self-pity and frustration every time I'm on my own and let myself think about what I'm missing out on.

Adam's visit was wonderful. After all the hassles finalising the arrangements and having not seen him for two and a half years, I was a bit worried about how we would respond to one another. Well, it was amazing: the family connection clicked in from day one and the communication level was better than that shared by good friends. Sherryl and all my other friends who came into contact with Adam during his visit have commented on what a great guy he has become. I agree and wrote today to tell him how proud I am to have him as my son.

Adam reminds me of myself at his age (19) in some respects, but I think he's got a lot more going for him – probably thanks to his mother. Setting aside different hairstyles and things (Adam has an earring and a tongue ring!) I looked a lot like he does now when I was that age. I was thinking along similar lines: I also wanted to get into film/television production; I also had liberal political views and I also was formulating views on life (I was amazed that Adam, like me at that age, was keeping a diary of his thoughts.)

What Adam has going for him is much greater self-confidence than I have ever had. A big difference between Adam and me relates to timing and I now realise that this was the main problem in trying to make arrangements for his visit. Whilst I am punctual and get uptight about making and keeping arrangements, Adam is really laid-back and perpetually late. This caused a few tiffs during his visit. I hope I have convinced him that, although getting uptight is useless, having some sense of urgency is important.

We had a great holiday together, which I've captured on video and Adam has edited. Sherryl, Adam's US friend Nick, Adam and I drove from Johannesburg to Plettenburg Bay via Beaufort West. En route, we visited the world-renowned Cango Caves as well as an animal sanctuary where we saw an array of game including crocodiles, alligators, and most of the big cats and we got to stroke cheetahs (more like dogs than cats, we were told.)

At Plett we shared a lovely double-storey, sea-view, house with three other families (a shifting total of about twenty-two of us when anyone was counting). We had access to rubber ducks, hobie cats, and 4x4s, but I have to confess that my buddies and I spent most of our time sitting on the beach, or sitting in pubs and restaurants, talking and drinking. The big teenage contingent played and partied like we used to do.

From Plett (Western Cape) to Umhlanga (Natal) via East London (Eastern Cape) where we dropped-off Sherryl. As usual, Umhlanga provided seaside fun. We also travelled inland to visit a game farm (mainly for American Nick's benefit) and saw a variety of wild-life including rhino and hippo. Then, back to Joburg, where Adam and I had the opportunity to spend some time together by ourselves and to discuss issues like maintenance. I hope he now has a better perspective on my position and on the fact that South Africa is not such a bad place if he does have to come back. Of course, I'd love to have Adam and Chris here with me, but I realise that that isn't what they want and isn't what is best for them if they can stay in the US. So I go on wishing them the opposite of what I would like for myself!"

Chapter 8
Life Goes On

Sherryl and I, with our friends Peter and Rose Karstel, had a great holiday in Thailand in October, 2001 (paid for by Peter's and my then employer company, Sage, as a reward for a capital raising project in which we had both been involved). A few days in Bangkok and then a week at a resort in Phuket. We hired two motor scooters in Phuket, which is a great way to get around. Even the girls had a go at riding the bikes as no licences had to be produced. Sherryl gave us all a fright by riding across a busy road before she remembered how to stop. I have a photo of me riding in the rain with Sherryl on pillion holding an umbrella over both of us: I had to keep telling her to lift it higher as I couldn't see the road! Fortunately, the drivers there are courteous and give tourists a wide berth. It is amazing to see whole families with bags and things on one scooter and often no helmets. We also made use of the ubiquitous three-wheeled tuk tuk taxis to get around; often scary as the drivers diced one another through the teeming traffic.

During 2002, both Adam and Chris with Dave (another US friend of Adam's) came out to South Africa and we had a fun time, including a visit to Sun City and the Pilansberg Game Reserve and another holiday at Umhlanga Rocks.

Chris and his girlfriend Megan visited late in December 2003. We had a super holiday with them, including a coastal stay at Plettenberg Bay with several other families with offspring of similar ages to Chris and Megan and a few days game viewing in the Kruger National Park. Another sad farewell which would have been even worse if I had known that it would be three and a half years before I would see my sons again. We did, however, stay in touch by e-mail and Skype.

During 2004, I owned the best and worst vehicles I have ever had. A couple of years before, I had bought *my second BMW*, a brand-new metallic silver BMW M3 (the second M3 model, which I still believe was the most stylish and a great car in every respect). In contrast to my Honda Prelude, I came to think of this car as a wolf in sheep's clothing as it was a five seater sedan that had prodigious performance. Whilst I had this car, I did a BMW driving course which enhanced my enjoyment of this and subsequent vehicles. I also made a few trips to Durban, particularly enjoying the car's acceleration from the tollbooths, its cornering ability through Van Reenan's Pass and even risking speeding fines (before average speed trapping in Natal) to push it towards its top speed.

Three friends and I purchased a plot of land in Bushwillow Estate adjacent to Vaalkop Dam and a nature reserve in the North West Province beyond Brits (about two and a half hours by car from Joburg). The access road and roads in the nature reserve were certainly not suitable for an M3 and so I bought *my first* 4x4, an old dark red Land Rover Discovery 2. I have never had as many breakdowns and punctures in any other vehicle, but did manage to do some off-road driving at Bushwillow as well as at a local 4x4 club and in the Natal Midlands and the Kruger National Park. Despite over time, having had to replace almost every part of the vehicle, it remained unreliable and I was glad to get rid of it. I subsequently also sold the M3 and replaced both of them with a good all-round vehicle: *my second* 4x4, a Toyota Fortuner diesel D4D, which I still have. Soon after buying it, I did an off-road driving course offered by Toyota and was very impressed with the vehicle's off-road capability. There was one occasion, however, when I got too cocksure and deep mud in the nature reserve adjacent to Bushwillow got the better of the vehicle. When I tried to drive through (using low ratio and diff lock) it got more bogged down and when I tried to reverse out it kept sliding into a fence (not good for the paintwork). Pulling it out with another vehicle also didn't work. The eventual solution involved Sherryl and her father and a couple of other guys pulling the car sideways with a rope to keep it away from the fence, while I reversed out of the mud patch. The Fortuner is a very practical vehicle: with the back seats in, it is a seven-seater people mover; with them out, it can carry a big load. With roof rack and bike rack, we use it to transport our canoes and mountain bikes and have used it to tow a trailer and a boat. It is comfortable on-road as well as off, and has taken us to many parts of southern Africa and to Mozambique. Surprisingly, however, given Toyota's famed reliability, the engine seized without warning or apparent reason when the vehicle was only two years old. Sherryl was driving up a steep hill when the engine cut out and would not restart. I put up a warning triangle, but we were in a dangerous position on a busy road. Fortunately, a family in another Toyota, towed us to the nearest garage where we had to wait for the AA tow truck. After some complaining by me, Toyota SA came to the party and paid some of the cost of the reconditioned engine.

At Bushwillow, we built a central boma (open-sided, horseshoe shaped structure of brick under thatch around a central braai area with kitchen, lounge, dining, bar and deck sections and boat shed/storeroom), plus four self-contained bedroom units in two separate cottages. "Motswiri", as we have called our place, is a great get-away from the city: in the heart of the Bushveld, with a variety of antelope, small game and birds coming right up to the boma for food and water and an even greater variety of game and birds in the nature reserve.

During 2005, we had enjoyable visits to South Africa from my brother and his wife and from my mother and her husband.

As if divorce and the "loss" of my sons were not enough for me to deal with, I was retrenched with effect from 28 February, 2006 from a job I had held for more than twenty years. Things had started to go wrong for the Sage Group a couple of years before, mainly as a result of expanding operations into the USA. What was supposedly going to be a 'virtual' insurance company in the US just kept growing and, with a worsening Rand/Dollar exchange rate and lack of support from the shareholders in the South African holding company resulting in ever more costly funding arrangements, it became apparent that the writing was on the wall for Sage. After the failure of a number of last-ditch efforts to save the

Group, Sage was sold to Momentum (another insurance group) and most of the Sage staff were retrenched.

Now I believed I had faced all the major traumas one person can experience: death (of my father, grandmother and several friends); nasty divorce; splitting up of my family (my brother to Australia, me to South Africa, my mother to the UK and my sons to the US); and retrenchment. Things could only get better – and fortunately did.

Because I was retrenched from Sage, I was allowed to take early retirement (aged fifty-four) and I used most of the money from my retrenchment package to augment my pension. This meant that, instead of trying to get back into the rat race (particularly difficult as an elderly, pale, male in the face of affirmative action), I could afford to take the chance to work from home as a legal consultant. I enjoyed the work, but it was feast or famine until I had a lucky break and got a retainer from iBurst Africa to be their in-house legal adviser on a part-time basis and mainly working from home. As another string to my bow, which I have not yet used, I was admitted as a member of the Chartered Institute of Arbitrators (London) in April 2007.

During May 2007, Sherryl and I had a fantastic holiday starting in the UK: London on our own and then Kendal in the Lake District with my mother and her husband. On to the US: New York City with my younger son and his girlfriend, Washington DC with my elder son and his girlfriend and then Florida with all four of them (the highlight being Disney World.)

Chapter 9
Marriage To Sherryl and Life In South Africa

Sherryl Myburgh, with whom I had had an up and down relationship for about twenty years, eventually agreed to marry me. We had bought our dream home in Douglasdale, Johannesburg and were living together. We had talked about marriage on numerous occasions and, at last, Sherryl had indicated that she might be ready to make the commitment.

During October, 2008, we had a short holiday at Hermanus on the Cape Coast with Sherryl's sister and brother-in-law (Gail and Andy Featherstone). After dinner one night, on a balcony with the sea on one side and mountains on the other, I went down on one knee and popped the question in traditional style. Sherryl said "Yes!" and I (temporarily) put my signet ring on her finger – I knew she would want to choose her own engagement ring.

Then came all the preparations for the wedding – including formally asking Sherryl's father for her hand in marriage, choosing the ring, an engagement party at our home, drawing up a budget, selecting a venue, deciding who to invite, hand-made invitations (Sherryl did those), arranging for a minister, photographers, cake, decor, flowers, outfits, wedding rings, gifts for the bridal party and guests, preparing speeches etc.

Arrangements were complicated by the fact that my family all live overseas. We had to arrange for their visits to this part of the world, accommodation, itineraries etc and, as my brother was to be my best man, I had to organise my own bachelor party.

The wedding was like a fairy tale. Saturday, 8 August, 2009 was a sunny winter's day, which was fortunate as the wedding ceremony took place in the open at a function venue on a bank of the Vaal River near Johannesburg. At midday, to the sounds of a lone piper, Sherryl, looking radiant in a traditional wedding dress with veil, was escorted by her father to stand beside me in front of our guests. The minister, a cousin of Sherryl's, opened the service with the words "At last!" which set the tone for a day of laughter and fun. The surprise for our ninety or so guests was that the reception was held on a large boat, which cruised along the river while we partied. The speeches went down well, especially my brother's speech as best man, which was hilarious: "Sherryl has spent over twenty years looking for a good man. Lucky for you, Stewart, that she didn't find one!"

Instead of going away for a honeymoon, Sherryl and I took the opportunity to spend the week after the wedding with our overseas visitors and friends. It was great to have all of Sherryl's and most of my close family members together for the first and only time. Unfortunately, my mother and George were unable to make the trip due to ill health.

Early the next year, I made the following diary note:
"Now that everything has gone back to normal and Sherryl and I have settled in to married life, I can honestly

say that I have never been happier. There were many times, particularly during and after the separation and divorce from Karen, when I doubted that I would ever again be truly happy. I realise that my current blissful state will not continue indefinitely. Life is a roller coaster with its ups and downs. But at least I now know that new heights can be reached."

As expected, there have been some downs as well as ups during the years since my marriage to Sherryl. We visited my Mum and George in England during July, 2010 and they had moved into sheltered housing in a rented council-owned flat on a river bank in Kendal. George had developed breathing problems and Mum arthritis. They had decided to move permanently to Perth, Australia, and had sold their house in the UK, but were unable to make the journey because Mum fell and broke her femur – after which her physical and mental health deteriorated rapidly. By the time of our visit, she was largely confined to bed at night and a chair in the lounge during the day, although she did take short walks in the corridor and we took her out in a wheelchair. Her short-term memory and reasoning powers had diminished, but she was still lucid and able to take part in our conversations. Despite George's worsening breathing difficulties, he seemed to revel in the role of caregiver to Mum and did everything for her. He was, however, very concerned about how she would cope after his death and he and I spent a lot of time arranging for completion of enduring powers of attorney, bank account and pension transfer forms etc.

On various visits to the UK, we have made quite a lot of use of trains and, of course, of the London Underground. On this trip, we experienced the Underground at its worst. We had to change trains a couple of times to get to Heathrow airport to catch our flight home. Sherryl and I each had a large suitcase plus I had a backpack and she had a carry bag. It was rush hour and there was a problem up the line, so all the trains were delayed. We were crowded like sardines on the platform and it was very hot and stuffy. The trains which came through were full, so eventually we had to join in the pushing, to squeeze into a carriage with our luggage and without losing one another. Hell on earth!

After Sherryl and I returned to South Africa, we were advised by George's son and daughter-in-law (Grahame and Aysha Harwood) that George had been admitted to hospital with fluid in his lungs and Marion had been put into a temporary care home. George died on 15th October, 2010. Sherryl and I (from Johannesburg, South Africa) and my brother and his wife (from Perth, Australia) flew to the UK to be with Mum. She died on 23rd October, 2010, just a week after the death of her beloved husband George.

There was a joint funeral service for Marion and George in Kendal on 12th November, 2010 (after George's autopsy), attended by Grahame and Aysha, George's daughter Louella and her husband Tony, and friends Mum and George had made in England. On the same day, we had a memorial service in Perth, Australia at the home of George's other daughter Moya, attended by Sherryl and me, Chris and Trish and their family, and friends Mum and George had made in Perth.

Sherryl and I had travelled to Perth for two happy family events: the wedding of Chris and Trish's son Matthew and the fortieth birthday party of Trish's son Steve, for which a big group of us went to Bali and had a fun holiday.

During 2011, I received an inheritance from the estates of my mother and stepfather and decided to treat myself to a sports car. With input from a 'petrol head' friend, I looked at various second-hand sports and super cars online, in magazines and showrooms. I soon realised that the recent model Lamborghinis and Ferraris were out of my price range. I thought I had found the ideal vehicle in the form of a 2010 Lotus Elise SC Supercharged, but when I took it for a test drive I soon realised it was simply too small for me. I'm tall so getting in and out was a problem and I felt cramped in the driver's seat. I also take size 12 shoes and the clutch and brake pedals were so close together that I had difficulty not pressing them both when I put in the clutch. I eventually decided on *my first sports car* (*owned*). A 2008 Porsche Boxster S Tiptronic with just 22,900 kilometres on the clock. It is metallic black with black electronic soft top and black leather upholstery and came with most of the bells and whistles: 18 inch light alloy wheels (silver), carbon ceramic brakes (red), limited slip differential, power steering, ABS, traction control, climate control, electric windows and mirrors and radio/CD player. As I bought the car from Porsche Centre, it also came with a two year/200,000 kilometre motor plan, new tyres, windscreen and mats, and re-sprayed paint work, as well as various Porsche gifts.

In August 2011, Sherryl and I eventually had our honeymoon and did one of the things on her 'bucket list.' We flew to Zanzibar and spent seven days at the Mapenzi Beach Club resort. Although we found the food disappointingly bland, the place was great and we had a fun trip on a dhow (a traditional Arab sailing vessel).

Chapter 10
Happy Holidays

"From London to LA with a wedding along the way" – the title of a coffee table photo book which provides a record of a memorable trip Sherryl and I made in October/November 2012. We flew from Joburg to Heathrow Airport, London, hired a car and drove to Kendal, the gateway to the Lake District. There we met up with family and friends to scatter the ashes of my late mother and stepfather on Scout Scar in Cumbria. It was a cold, wet and windy day and, although it was a sad occasion, there were some humorous moments – such as when my brother tipped some of the ashes out of one of the containers and a gust of wind blew them back all over him and he said, "I wonder whether they'll let me back into Australia carrying human remains."

Sherryl and I spent a few days exploring the historic city of York, including York Minster, Clifford's Tower and the York Castle Museum. Back to London where we took in a musical at a West End Theatre. Next stop was New York, where we stayed with my son Chris in his apartment in Upper East Manhattan, which we were told by our cab driver was a very good address, but which did have its shortcomings. On the top (fifth) floor of a building with no lift! We met up with my brother Chris and Trish for sightseeing: the city with its skyscrapers and yellow cabs, the Flat Iron building, St Patrick's Cathedral, the Top of the Rock with its magnificent views of the city, Broadway, Central Park, the Statue of Liberty and so on. Sherryl had entered to take part in the New York City Marathon, but unfortunately the event was cancelled at the last minute due to Hurricane Sandy.

The marriage of my younger son Chris to Megan took place in the city of Baltimore and we went there by train from New York during a snowstorm. In American tradition, we went to the rehearsal dinner the night before the wedding. The wedding and reception took place at a very smart country club and were arranged by my ex-wife Karen and her husband Derek. My elder son Adam was best man and the guests included my brother and his wife.

Sherryl and I then flew to Los Angeles to spend time visiting Adam and his girlfriend Lindsay. They rent a house with a sea view at Playa del Rey and showed us some of LA's many attractions. In LA, we met up again with Chris and Trish who had hired a Ford Mustang convertible. We took a drive with them in the Mustang and went, amongst other places, to Rodeo Drive, where I took a photo of a black and yellow Bugatti Veyron. We had lunch at Hooters and paid a visit to Grauman's Chinese Theatre and the famous street with hand and foot prints of the stars. Adam works for a film production company in Hollywood and arranged for us to have a tour of Paramount Pictures. He drove an old red Jeep which he was in the process of doing up. The Jeep is open to the elements and it was cold in LA so I have a photo of Sherryl wearing running gloves on her feet (over her sandals) as we were driving to the beach!

Next Sherryl and I did a trip which was billed as the "Best of the West" and was definitely a highlight. Using a combination of a small plane (twenty seater) and coaches, we visited all the following places over a ten day period:

- Monterey, where we took a boat trip in the bay.
- The famous Pebble Beach golf course and Carmel.
- San Francisco, where we visited Alcatraz, the Golden Gate Bridge and Lombard Street (the most crooked street in the world).
- Muir Woods National Park.
- Sonoma, where we did wine and cheese tastings.
- Sausalito.
- Yosemite National Park, with its giant Sequoias and Redwoods.
- Zion National Park.
- Bryce Canyon National Park.
- Grand Canyon National Park (we found Bryce Canyon with its pinnacles even more spectacular than the Grand Canyon).
- Las Vegas, where we saw the volcano at the Mirage, the fountains at Caesar's Palace and took a gondola ride at the Venetian.

We were able to fit in so much because we would fly to a place where a coach would be waiting on the runway. We would then be taken on a tour, delivered to a hotel where our luggage was already in our room, stay over, and then move on to the next place. We met a variety of people. Most of the others on the tour were Chinese and, once they realised they had to keep to the schedule, they were charming travelling companions. There was also a Scottish couple from the same small town my parents once lived in and "the awful Ozzies" as we dubbed them: two elderly Australian ladies who complained about everything, especially the tardiness of the Chinese. The air hostess on the plane was a character who kept us entertained in a Southern drawl and the coach drivers included a Pommy transvestite and a good ole boy with a rattle snake jaw on his Stetson.

***

During August, 2013, Sherryl and I drove in my Porsche to Umhlanga Rocks on the KwaZulu Natal coast. Being mid-engined, the car has luggage space at the front and the back, so you can fit in much more than you would expect of a sports car. After a week of enjoying the attractions of Umhlanga and surrounds and driving with the top down, we took the long route to East London via Underberg with many long hilly bends to enjoy the car's road holding, and overtaking opportunities to enjoy its acceleration. We had a short holiday with Sherryl's mother in Gonubie, East London, the highlight of which was a flip in a helicopter. We drove out to the East London airport where we were introduced to our pilot, a very pleasant Black guy who joked about having just got his taxi licence. He flew us back to Gonubie, flying low, right over Sherryl's mother's house, then landing on a patch of grass between the Gonubie hotel and the beach. We felt like film stars getting out of the helicopter and going for a walk along the boardwalk before getting back in and taking off – with lots of people pointing, commenting and taking photos.

In February, 2014, Sherryl and her sister Gail and I drove to the world-famous Kruger National Park in my Toyota Fortuner to meet up with Gail's husband Andy, who was already in the Park on a birding expedition. We took the long drive on mainly dirt roads from Malelane Gate to Lower Sabi. The game viewing en route was amongst the best I have experienced. At one point, we were stopped in the road looking at giraffe near the side of the vehicle and I happened to look in my rear-view mirror and saw a white rhino just behind us. We had one hair-raising experience where we came to a low-level bridge over which the river was flowing. I had no way of measuring the depth in the middle nor the strength of the current, but it was a very long way to turn back. So I took what could have proven to be a stupid risk and drove slowly across the bridge. After we arrived at our destination, my vehicle started to misfire. When we drove from one camp to another, it got worse and I phoned and booked it in for a service at a Toyota service station in Hazyview, the town nearest the Kruger Park (about sixty kilometres away). However, as we drove towards Skukuza Camp to exit the park, the chugging got worse and worse. I couldn't get out of second gear and really battled to get uphill. At one point there were elephant on the road, but I did not want to stop the vehicle in case it conked out so I tooted and kept going, and fortunately they moved out of the way. I realised there was no way we were going to get to Hazyview, but I remembered there was a vehicle workshop at Skukuza (where I had previously taken my Land Rover Discovery to have a puncture repaired). So, I pulled in there and explained my predicament to the mechanic. He asked whether I had travelled a long way on dirt roads and when I confirmed this, he said he knew what the problem was – some sensor that protects the engine against dust – in a 4x4! Anyway, he replaced a bolt and the car ran normally. I asked how much I owed him and he said whatever I wanted to pay. So I gave him R200 and he seemed happy. Although, on reflection, I should have given him more – as, had I got the vehicle to Hazyview, I'm sure it would have cost at least R2 000.

***

"From Auckland to WA with a wedding along the way" – the proposed title of a second coffee table photo book that we have not yet got around to putting together. During November/December 2015, Sherryl and I did a trip which included almost every type of motorised transport. A friend gave us a lift in his car to Montecasino (a casino and entertainment complex near where we live), from where we took a bus to the Gautrain station in Sandton. From there, by fast train to OR Tambo Airport to catch a flight to Auckland, New Zealand via Perth, Australia. We came close to not being able to board the flight and had hassles all along the way as the travel agent (Flight Centre) had issued my wife's ticket in the name Sherryl Elaine without adding her surname, Cant, and we had not noticed!

We spent an enjoyable week with Sherryl's half-brother, Grant, and his wife, Rachel, and their two young daughters, Catherine and Elizabeth. Our sightseeing included taking a ferry from Devonport to the City and visiting the Viaduct; taking a boat to Waikheke Island and visiting Mudbrick Wine Farm – where we enjoyed wine tasting and a wonderful degustation menu; and travelling by car to Piha beach with its black sand. On one of the days in Auckland, Sherryl and I took the girls (then aged six and three) to the local museum and managed to lose our car. Whilst Sherryl was running around the park looking for it, I was left to look after the little girls (not something I have done before, having sons not daughters). Much to my consternation, the younger one, Elizabeth, told me she needed to go to the toilet. I was very concerned about moving away from where Sherryl had left us and did not know what, if any, assistance Elizabeth would require and therefore whether to take her to a ladies or gents toilet. Fortunately, Sherryl came to the rescue.

From Auckland we flew to Wellington where we had planned to stay for two nights, but could only get accommodation for one night – due, we discovered, to an Elton John concert. Whilst in Wellington, we took the cable car to the Botanic Garden and also visited Cuba Street. The next morning we took the Interislander Ferry to Picton. The accommodation we got there was different to say the least. A single room with a glassed-in shower in one corner and a toilet with a low partition in another corner! From Picton we travelled on Kiwi Rail to Christchurch. A relaxing trip, during which you can take in the varied and spectacular scenery through the big carriage windows or from the open viewing car (too cold) or the lounge car (a beer in hand, ideal). In addition to the scenery, we saw a procession of vintage cars driving on the road alongside the railway line. In Christchurch, we visited the magnificent Botanic Gardens with the punters in straw boaters and striped blazers on the Avon River, had a ride on a motorised tram and took a trip on an open-top bus from which we were shown the terrible damage done by the 2010/2012 earthquakes.

We had arranged to hire a campervan in Christchurch. When we went to collect it we were asked whether we wanted to take out rollover insurance. My reaction was "no", until the hire company rep explained that high winds had caused four of their vehicles to roll over during the past month. Needless to say, we took the insurance! We drove in the campervan to Queenstown where we had a stop-over and then to Milford Sound via Lake Takapo and Te Anau. The scenery in New Zealand is spectacular, with a photo opportunity around every corner. Sea and sand, huge unspoiled lakes, flowing rivers, snow-capped mountains, green fields and an abundance of interesting and colourful flora and fauna. Campervans are a popular and enjoyable way to see the country, with excellent amenities at all the campsites. On the South Island, however, allow for the journeys to take much longer than you are used to. Driving a big, slow vehicle, which is being buffeted by the wind, along narrow, winding, hilly roads takes some getting used to and progress is slow, particularly if, like us, you keep stopping to admire the scenery and take photos.

There is very little at Milford Sound except the campsite and boat harbour. We took a day trip through the Sound on a large Catamaran. The water is surrounded by mountains and, with a grey sky overhead, somewhat eerie. There are lots of waterfalls and the prow of the boat was driven right under the waterfall in a couple of places. We had booked to spend two nights at Milford Sound but heard that a big storm was expected the next day. We did not fancy driving back up through the mountain pass in a storm and so checked out early and drove back and spent a night at Te Anau. From there, back to Queenstown for two nights. We took the cable car up the mountain and at the top Sherryl braved a ride on the luge. On departure day, we had to watch other campers to see how to dispose of the waste from the campervan before returning it.

From Queenstown, we flew back to Auckland and spent a few more days with Sherryl's brother and his family. We celebrated an early Christmas with them: decorating the tree, shopping and exchanging gifts and having a traditional Christmas dinner.

We then flew to Perth, Australia, and spent a few days with my brother Chris and his wife Trish at their lovely home in Hilarys. We were there to attend the wedding of their daughter, Emma Cant, to Daniel Wurst (known as "Wursty"). Chris and I attended Wursty's bachelor party, which was quite an eye-opener. We met up with the other guys at a laser paintball field, where we had a few beers and then waited in the car park. A long, black van with blacked out (one-way glass) windows and fat tyres on fancy silver rims pulled up. Out of the driver's seat stepped an attractive young woman wearing a revealing black pantsuit and a driver's cap over her long blonde hair. She opened the sliding side door of the van, and, standing in the doorway, was a gorgeous redhead wearing not a stitch of clothing. She welcomed us into the van, which had music videos showing on the back wall of the cab. We were a bit cramped sitting along the two sides and back of the van and initially I, and I think some of the others, were somewhat embarrassed. But "Mandy" was totally relaxed, friendly and chatty, did some dancing, handed out beers, drank some champagne and sat on various laps. I thought it would be a strictly 'no touch' affair, but one of the guys asked if her boobs were real and she invited him to feel and decide for himself, then admitted she had had a boob job. At one stage on the drive to Fremantle, we stopped to buy more beers and make a pit stop. When the side door opened briefly, some senior school kids obviously got a glimpse of the contents of the van and by the time we pulled out there was quite a crowd of them trying to see in! We were dropped off at a pub in Freo and Mandy (now dressed) climbed into a big, new Mercedes-Benz, so appears to be earning good money. At the pub we had more drinks and played some pool and then took Uber cabs back home.

We drove with Chris and Trish to Silver Pines in Cowaramup for the wedding, billed by the bride and groom as the "Cant get Wurst Wedding". We spent a couple of days before and after the wedding at Silver Pines which is a working farm and function venue. We stayed in a cottage with the bride and various family members and the groom and his family were in another cottage. Guests were in camper vans, caravans and tents. The whole thing was one big, festive party, marred only by the flies, which were unbearable unless you stayed inside with closed door and window screens.

Back in Perth, we visited the beautiful Kings Park, the Lucky Shag Waterfront Bar, Millbrook Wine Estate and historic Jarrahdale. For the return flight, we were lucky enough to get an upgrade to business class and, for the first time, experienced full flat seats.

My elder son Adam proposed to his American girlfriend, Lindsay, on the beach in Zanzibar during September, 2015, after which they spent a few days with us in Joburg. Because of the brevity of their visit, and the fact that Lindsay had not been here before, we did a Red Bus tour of the City with hop on and off stops at various places of interest. It was great fun and Sherryl and I saw parts of Joburg we had not been to for many years, and a few places we had not been to at all. We also took a trip out to the Hartebeespoort Dam and went up the mountain in the cable car. At the top, there are spectacular views as well as walks and restaurants. On the way back, we had lunch at the Neck and Deck Restaurant, where we fed giraffe from the deck and viewed a variety of local and exotic game. I wanted to give Adam and Lindsay a drive in my Porsche – problem with this is that it is strictly a two seater; so he and I drove out to Gilroy's pub and brewery in the Porsche followed by Lindsay and Sherryl in my Toyota Fortuner. After lunch (limited beers as I had to drive back), we swapped vehicles for the drive home. Adam brought with him an expensive and impressive drone fitted with a camera. As noted previously, I have long had a desire to fly some sort of aircraft and it struck me that flying a drone is now the closest I'm likely to get. So I did some research and my sons bought me, for my birthday, a relatively cheap quadcopter fitted with a camera and FPV (first person view) meaning you can theoretically fly it whilst getting a pilot's eye view on the control screen. The problem is that the one I got is so light that it changes direction with every gust of wind; so nearly impossible to fly at all, never mind using FPV!

"From Washington to LA with a wedding along the way" is the proposed title of a third coffee table book we want to put together, with photos of our trip to the USA during March/April 2016. We flew to Washington DC (Dulles International Airport) via London; a long flight made even longer by a two hour queue to clear customs and immigration at Dulles. My younger son Chris and his wife Megan had moved from New York to Washington and bought a house in Rockville. We had a great visit with them and got to meet our grandson, Owen, who was just five- months-old and is a real cutie. Megan's mother had loaned them her car (a Jeep Grand Cherokee), so the five of us (including baby seat and paraphernalia) were able to get around in one vehicle. We visited the famous Arlington Cemetery, had lunch at an Irish pub on St Patrick's Day and wine tastings at various vineyards and meals at various restaurants. We took a walk while it was snowing (a first for Sherryl), and visited George Washington's house. On a workday for Chris, Sherryl and I took the tube into Washington and explored the Smithsonian Air and Space Museum. We had lunch at a café, which was unbearably hot inside, so we decided to sit at an outside table in our winter woollies. A gust of wind blew over an umbrella which hit me on the head, but fortunately did no damage. America, being the litigious country it is, the manager was of course very concerned and gave us our meal and drinks for free. Imagine how much more concerned he would have been had he known I was a lawyer! We also experienced a Maryland speciality at Megan's parents' house: a "Crab Feast," where you sit at a plastic covered table with a wooden hammer which you use to pulverise a mountain of crabs to get the meat out – hard work for relatively little reward but good fun.

If our experience was anything to go by, never use American Airlines! We were booked to fly from Washington Reagan Airport to San Jose Cabo in Mexico in order to attend Adam's wedding. I have a British passport and Sherryl has a South African passport. I had checked online that neither of us needed a visa for Mexico as we both had visas for the USA. Fortunately, we got to the airport early, as the first thing that happened was that the automatic check-in machine would not issue Sherryl's boarding pass and the readout stated we needed to get assistance. We eventually found a woman who took Sherryl's passport and disappeared. Time was running out when she eventually returned and said Sherryl needed a visa for Mexico. Fortunately, I had the printout from my online enquiries and showed her that that was not correct. She said we needed to go to the resolutions desk. This was cordoned off, so we ducked under the cordon and joined the queue. Now time was really running out and we reluctantly agreed on a deadline for Chris and I to go ahead (as best man and father of the groom) and leave poor Sherryl to sort things out. Thankfully, we got to the front of the queue before the deadline and, after being shown my printout and consulting a manager, the assistant issued Sherryl's boarding pass. Chris ran with our two heavy suitcases to the baggage check-in, and we only just made it onto the flight.

We hired a SUV and drove through the town of San Jose Del Cabo and out to the beach area, where we dropped off Sherryl at the bed and breakfast establishment we had booked. Chris and I then drove to Cabo San Lucas to attend the stag night. Chris had booked a suite in a luxury hotel and we met up with Adam and three of his friends there. Cabo San Lucas is a 'party town' and, as our visit coincided with US school Spring Break, was chock full of young, scantily clad American teenagers. We had dinner at a restaurant on the beach, drinks at various pubs and ended up at a strip joint. Somewhat hungover, we drove back to San Jose Del Cabo the next day. The area is spectacular with a desert landscape (reminiscent of old cowboy movies) running down to unspoiled beaches and the sea. The wedding party stayed in a luxurious villa, with wedding guests staying at other villas, hotels and bed and breakfast establishments in the area. We had a few days of partying, including the US traditional wedding rehearsal dinner. The wedding ceremony took place on the beach in front of the villa and the reception was in the grounds of the villa. On the day after the wedding, we all drove to Flora Farms for their Easter brunch. This place is like a green oasis in the middle of the desert and serves a magnificent brunch, with platter after platter of Mexican-style food, jugs of ice-cold Margaritas and Bloody Marys decorated with fruit and garnish. Sherryl and I also took the opportunity to explore the old town and buy some gifts and mementos.

Chris had left the previous day with the hired SUV, so we had to squeeze into Adam's hired sedan for the trip back to the airport – no mean feat for four of us with lots of luggage. We flew to LA and spent a few very enjoyable days with Adam and Lindsay and their dog Kona, doing drives and walks. A highlight was taking the ferry to Catalina Island and exploring the island in a golf cart and on foot. Then it was time to fly back to Joburg via London. Although we had booked through

British Airways, the first leg was a code share with American Airlines and another near disaster. This time the check-in machine would not issue my boarding pass. We eventually found an assistant who asked to see my visa to enter South Africa. I showed her the South African permanent resident stamp in my British passport, but she said there was not enough information. I asked what she meant and she said "there is no expiry date." My angry reply was *"Do you know what permanent means?"* My wife got me to calm down and a manager was called who issued my boarding pass. The contrast between the first leg of our flight (on AA) and the second leg (on BA) was huge. On the first leg, there was less legroom, scruffy looking, disinterested air hostesses and inferior food. Subsequently, I have written to BA suggesting they no longer code share with AA.

At the time of writing this (August 2016), the world appears to be in a state of socio-political upheaval. Brexit (Britain exiting the European Union) and Donald Trump being the Republican candidate for President of the USA reveal an unfortunate and inevitable consequence of democracy – even those opposed to democracy and the principles associated with it (such as non-racism) get the vote. The reaction of ordinary people to the atrocities perpetrated by ISIS and other extremist groups is certainly understandable, but unfortunately extends all too readily to general xenophobia. I used to think that Britain was one of the few countries in the world where democracy worked, but Brexit calls this into question. Not only has it harmed Britain's economy in the short-term and will probably have various adverse consequences in the long-term, but it has already led to racial intolerance and hostility on an unprecedented scale. Trump's candidacy and rhetoric (building a wall to keep out Mexicans etc.) are currently widely regarded as a joke, but it could be a very bad joke indeed were he to become US President. Africa has seen many examples of democracy failing: one-man one-vote one-time has regrettably been the case in most countries after getting independence. A rabble-rouser gets the vote on the basis of promises which he cannot fulfil, and then does everything he can to stay in power – including destroying any real democracy, or is ousted from power and replaced by a dictator or oligarchy.

When the ANC under Nelson Mandela was voted into power in South Africa, I, and I think most of my fellow countrymen, were very optimistic about the future of our 'rainbow nation.' However, with the advent of Jacob Zuma and the rampant corruption in the country, I began to think South Africa was on the same slippery slope as Zimbabwe under Robert Mugabe. Recently, however, there have been some beacons of hope. Our institutions, in particular the Courts and the Public Protector (Thuli Madonsela) have withstood political pressure and upheld the principles of democracy. For example, the High Court ruling that Zuma should face corruption charges (stemming from the 1999 arms deal) and the Public Protector ruling (upheld by the Constitutional Court) that he must pay back the money (public funds improperly used to pay for non-security upgrades at his Nkandla homestead). And many of the voters in the recent local government elections have shown their dissatisfaction with the ANC Government. More important, unlike in Zimbabwe, these challenges to the President and the

Government have been allowed to happen. It is ironic, but certainly a cause for optimism, that South Africa is now one of the few countries in the world where democracy appears to be working!

Since writing the foregoing, there have been some unfortunate developments. Much to the surprise and consternation of many people in America and worldwide, Trump will be the next President of the USA. I think the following quote from Winston Churchill is apposite: "The best argument against democracy is a five-minute conversation with the average voter." Sadly it appears that not only is democracy not working anywhere in Africa (not even here in South Africa despite my earlier optimism), but it is also not working in the UK or the USA. I believe the only solution may lie in a concept which is currently not 'politically correct' – a qualified franchise. Give everybody one vote, but give additional votes based on stipulated qualifications such as level of education, savings, home ownership, employment, employment of others, no criminal record, tax status. Of course, equal opportunity should be a prerequisite to such a system. But the purpose would be to limit the power of those who, for whatever reason, have not taken advantage of the opportunities provided to them and who make no meaningful contribution to the society they live in.

***

During October 2016 Sherryl and I had a fun road trip. We drove in my Toyota Fortuner from Joburg to a resort near the Gariep Dam in the Free State. After an overnight stay, we drove to the Addo Elephant Park in the Eastern Cape, where we stayed for two nights. On a self-game drive on the first evening we saw nothing but two buffalo so thought this place would be a disappointment. But, on the following two days, we saw lots of buffalo, elephant, mountain zebra, warthog and black-backed jackal. Because of the drought South Africa was then experiencing, there was very little water in the waterholes and we even saw rangers digging at a waterhole to bring water to the surface, surrounded by thirsty buffalo and warthog!

From there we drove to St. Francis Bay and spent two nights with an old friend who has a beautiful home on the golf estate. She is a keen birder and showed us some Denham bustards – the males making an impressive display of their chest feathers to attract the females. We then drove down to Plettenberg Bay where we spent four nights in a resort up on a hill overlooking the town and the bay. Variable weather, but we did have a morning on the beach, a visit to Robberg Nature Reserve and some good lunches and dinners at various restaurants. We also visited ex-Joburg friends who now live in Knysna.

From Plett, we drove to Oudshoorn, famed for its ostrich farms. We spent two nights in a lovely B&B and Sherryl and some friends ran the Meiringspoort half marathon. This entailed driving to a small town called De Rust, which was invaded by more than 2000 runners and their families. The runners climbed into cattle trucks, which took them to the start near the Meiringspoort waterfall, then ran back to De Rust. I walked around the village, had breakfast at a roadside restaurant and then watched the runners streaming into the finish. Later that day, we drove to Calitzdorp and did wine tasting at Boberg Winery and had lunch at De Krans Winery. These are both on Route 62 and we have decided that is a must-do for the future. We drove home from Oudshoorn in one day as Sherryl had to work the next day. Eleven and a half hours of travelling – only manageable because each of us drove in two hour stints, but not something I would readily do again. Very impressed with my Fortuner which gave no trouble at all.

Chapter 11
A Message of Hope

In looking back at the diary I kept from the time my first marriage started falling apart until the time of my second marriage, I realised that I am in a position to share a message of hope. Extracts from my diary reveal just how bad I felt over various developments.

9th March, 1987

"Then Karen cracks and turns the tables – threatens me with divorce and I suddenly realise how much I have to lose. I don't really accept much of what she is saying but I feel that I can't live without her. I feel jealousy, fear of even greater loneliness, disappointment, frustration and bitterness at the seeming waste of time and effort and a desperate desire to keep my children. Nobody else is going to have what is mine, what is so perfect, in whom I have such pride and for whom I feel so strongly, so protective, so possessive. And I don't want to lose my home and my possessions and my planned holiday and everything we've worked for and should be enjoying and looking forward to."

12th March, 1987

"Karen keeps saying the ball is in my court and I have to inspire affection in her. However, not only does she refuse to make any positive contribution, but she is hardly allowing me any opportunity and those efforts I have made don't seem to be changing things. But, when I point this out and ask what I'm doing wrong or what I should be doing, she says she has already spent a whole year telling me and refuses to say more. I don't know what to do."

6th October, 1987

"Despite all my efforts, the crunch of separation came about. On Sunday, 4th October, 1987, I moved out of the family home and left this note for Karen:

Dear Karen,

I have never felt so sad and lonely in my life. You and the boys are my family and my friends; without you all, everything seems meaningless. I realise that my plight is my problem and largely my fault. But unfortunately, I cannot undo the mistakes of the past. All I can do is offer you all a future in which I would be guided by a realisation of my past mistakes. A future in which I would never take anything for granted again – suddenly every little thing that the boys do, every little home comfort seem hugely important. But my feelings extend well beyond a comfort zone for myself – I also want to provide everything I possibly can for you and the boys, not just material things but also emotional support and affection. The point is that I love you all in every sense of the word and will miss you unbearably. I only pray that the separation will be as short as possible.

All my love

Stewart."

7th November, 1987

"I feel that God has let me down. I have prayed so long and so hard for help in saving my marriage. Tonight was "make or break" and the "make" never even got a look in. I don't know what to do now. Do I really deserve this? I wish someone would kill me and save me from having to contemplate doing it myself. I'm slowly numbing my brain with alcohol – it's not what I want, but who gives a fuck about anything? I'm definitely feeling sorry for myself, but why shouldn't I? What have I got? No accessible family, no close friends, no lady friends, no confidence! I'm too old, tired, shy, and set in my ways to go right back to square one. I look around and feel envious of people I used to feel sorry for as not having as much as I thought I had. I have fantastic sons, but now on a part-time basis. I had a fantastic wife, but apparently never again. And I don't have the confidence, contacts, or even desire, to replace all that."

30th December, 1987

"I'm writing this at a friend's house in Harare, Zimbabwe, and I am feeling close to tears. Being in Zimbabwe again has brought memories flooding back, especially today. I drove out with my sons to visit my

Dad's grave. That brought back some sad childhood memories, but even those were overshadowed by comparison with my present situation. I showed the boys places where I spent my childhood and teenage years. But much more poignant were the reminders of the early years of my marriage to Karen. I took the boys to see a cottage in Avondale – Adam's first home and Karen's and my last home in Zimbabwe. We drove along avenues on which Karen and I had spent hours walking and talking, particularly when we were considering moving to South Africa. How I wished to be able to go back to that kind of sharing of plans with her. The boys and I had ice creams at the Dairy Den on Second Street, something we had done as a family just this time last year, and yet, it seems so distant. I saw an old Alfa Romeo similar to the car I had in Zims. And, shortly afterwards, I saw a Triumph Spitfire – Karen's car for most of our time together in Zims; the car in which we travelled to South Africa; and Karen's car for our first few months in Johannesburg."

28th January, 1988

"God, I'm unhappy. Not constantly, because I can mask the hurt by throwing myself into other activities: drinking, exercise, work, socialising, organising – even by concentrating on the anger and resentment I feel. But, on analysis, it all seems so pointless – living a charade and hoping and praying for a miracle that seems ever less likely to happen. Will I ever be happy again? Really happy? Even when I'm on my own and thinking about things? In the absence of a miracle which saves our marriage, I find it difficult to believe I could ever be truly happy again because it seems there must always be that sense of loss and of failure and the need to make comparisons with what has gone before. All I can do is to pray (yet again) for a miracle. As a first choice a miracle which will save our marriage and, as an alternative, one which will enable me to find happiness with someone else. Will I ever read this and realise that one of those miracles has happened and that I was being melodramatic in writing it? Pray, God, that will be the case and as soon as may be possible."

30th January, 1988

"If it weren't for Adam and Chris, I think I could kill myself. Fortunately, I don't have the courage, but I do now understand why and how people are driven to suicide. There can't be a worse situation than being unable to prevent the destruction of everything you are living for."

2nd May, 1989

"Will I ever be truly happy again? It seems that nobody I find can fill the void in my life that Karen has left. After all, she was an integral part of my life from my days at Varsity to my late thirties – from Zimbabwe to South Africa (with Europe and Canada en route); from single to married with two children; from student to businessman; from old Ford Cortina to new Mercedes-Benz; from long, brown hair to balding, short, greying hair; from loneliness back to loneliness".

27th September 1989

"I had a note from Karen yesterday signed "K. A. Woodhouse" (her maiden name) to remind me of the requirement to increase the maintenance. It's strange to think that it's finally all over, except for the products of our relationship in the form of Adam and Chris. That a phase of my life that took me from my early 20s as a University student in Zimbabwe - through countless experiences including engagement, marriage, childbirth X 2, holidays in Durban and Britain, a trip to Canada, a move to Johannesburg, and purchase of our own home – to my late 30s as a corporate legal adviser in Johannesburg, has come to an end. Almost two decades spanning the prime years of my life have become a closed book instead of an ongoing series."

7th May, 1997

"I am distraught. My main concern at present is that I am about to lose my sons. Having had them with me every second weekend and long school holidays during the whole time since my separation from Karen, it is hard to accept that they will be moving to the US a few months from now. That means that, at best, they will spend a few weeks each year with me for the next few years. I can understand why people commit suicide or even murder. If you can't, you haven't experienced the kinds of problems I have or you are a much stronger person. Take murder – I'm pretty sure it's beyond me to do it, but I can empathise with someone who commits a crime of passion. I walk in and find my wife or girlfriend *in flagrante delicto* (legalese for "fucking someone else") and bang, bang – they both get their just desserts. Suicide is even easier for me to relate to. Again, I think it's beyond me to actually do it. But I'm hurting and I believe I have little to live for, so why not end it?"

Various developments during the decade from 1987 to 1997 had me feeling deeply depressed, doubting whether I would ever again find real happiness, and even contemplating suicide. Thereafter things gradually improved to the point when I can now say that I have found even greater happiness than I have ever felt before. I found and am now married to my true soul mate and we have a wonderful life together. My sons have taken the opportunity to make good lives for themselves in the USA. Although I wish we could spend more time together, we have had some splendid holidays together and Sherryl and I were able to attend both their weddings and to meet our grandson. And we will, I hope, spend more time together in the not too distant future. Of course, even after my down decade, there have been (and will be) further downs as well as ups on the roller coaster of life. But if you're going through a bad patch and feeling down, I can tell you from personal experience that you can get through it and that there will be an upside. Maybe, like me, you'll be lucky enough to soar to even greater heights than you reached before the big dip.

Chapter 12
Looking Backwards

I share the Aristotelian notion that "happiness is the meaning and purpose of life, the whole aim and end of human existence." So, what have I learned about achieving happiness in the sixty-five years of my existence? What pearls of wisdom do I have to share? Nothing unique or original I'm afraid, but I have come to believe that there are **Four Pillars of Happiness:**

1. **Health**

Fitness (physical and mental) or at least good health is a prerequisite to full enjoyment of anything. Most of us take our health for granted and only really appreciate its importance when we are unwell. Unfortunately, injury or disease can strike us down despite our best efforts to avoid them, but that does not mean there is nothing we can do to reduce the risks. Obvious do's and don'ts of which from time to time we need to remind ourselves: Do not do drugs, smoke cigarettes, overdo alcohol, or take stupid risks. Do exercise (body and mind), watch diet, and practice safe sex. Of course these things are easier said than done. Although I have never taken illegal drugs and managed to give up smoking many years ago, I have battled for most of my adult life to control my alcohol intake and have often lost the battle and done things I regret, including taking stupid risks like driving drunk or having unprotected sex with a stranger. I have also battled with my weight as I really enjoy eating and drinking, but I have compensated to some extent by plenty of physical exercise – I currently do an hour of varied exercise six days a week. I have managed to lose weight despite bulking up, the main secret to which appears to be a six monthly testosterone injection, which was recommended by my GP about two years ago.

2. Love

Love, or at least companionship, is for most of us another prerequisite to enjoyment. To me, travel with a partner or friend is a joy, but on my own a bore. Again, the fickle finger of fate sometimes decrees that we lose loved ones or companions, but again there are things we can do to reduce the risks. One of the most important lessons I have learned is never to take your partner for granted – something that is easy to do but not to undo. Once you have lost your partner, for whatever reason, you cannot put back the clock no matter how much you wish you could do so. I ended up divorced from my first wife and nearly ended up splitting up with my current wife long before we got married. Although I do not accept all the blame, especially for my divorce, I do acknowledge that I was largely responsible for driving my first wife and my lady friend into the arms of others through taking them for granted, and thinking I could go on drinking to excess and flirting with other women.

Friends may come and go, but if you want to have ongoing companionship, you constantly have to work at building and maintaining relationships. Maybe I'm not as popular as I would like to think I am, but it often seems to me that I am the one who has to do the 'running' to maintain my friendships. Many of my friends and acquaintances accept my invitations, go along with my suggestions, eventually answer my e-mails, but generally do not initiate anything much themselves. I used to respond on a "tit-for-tat" basis; my turn, your turn, but soon realised that I was losing contact with people I like. We're all different and so what if I seem to be making more effort than others.

3. Wealth

Wealth may not be something we all desire, but we all need at least adequate resources to do the things we want to do. "Money cannot buy happiness", but it can help! Making money is easy, but only if you have money to start with. Starting out is the problem and I can do no better than refer young people to the books by Robert Kiyosaki, starting with "Rich Dad Poor Dad". His "cash flow quadrant" is the foundation:

| E stands for Employee | B stands for Business owner |
| S stands for Self-employed | I stands for Investor |

On the left side of the Quadrant, employees and self-employed individuals represent earning money on your own, as an individual. This means that your income potential is finite, limited to your own ability and your personal time to perform. There are only so many hours in a day. However, successful people on the right side of the quadrant operate as a team. They form their own networks for success. Their income potential is infinite because it is based on other people's time and other people's money working for them. If I'd had Kiyosaki's practical advice, I do not think it would have taken most of my life and a lot of luck to work my way from E to I. Once you are an investor, it is relatively easy to grow your investments based on the two **Keys to Investment:**

1. Diversify – Four Pillars of Investment: shares, cash, property, offshore.
2. Time –time in the market, not timing the market.

4. **Attitude**

One of the keys to happiness is a positive attitude: "the glass is half full rather than half empty" (Unknown).

If you want to find fault you will find it. I have a friend who invariably finds something to complain about when we go to a restaurant: everything can be great, but he will send back a fork with a speck of dirt on it. That sort of negativity can unnecessarily spoil the occasion for my friend, his companions and the waiter. I'm not saying that we should not complain when something is wrong; in fact, South Africans are generally too reluctant to complain. But let's keep the complaints for serious problems. Most of us are also too stingy with our praise. How much happier an occasion for all if my friend wiped the fork himself, complimented the chef on the food and thanked the waiter for good service.

"Remember yesterday, dream about tomorrow, but live today" (John D Rockefeller III). That is good advice for most people, myself included. Some of us dwell in the past, like those who try to relive their schooldays through reminiscing and old-boy reunions, or through their children. Others spend most of their time looking forward to the weekend or to their next holiday. I'm inclined to do both, especially when I'm on my own. When I am out walking by myself, I'm so lost in thought about what I should have said to someone or about what I'm going to tell someone, that I'm not really experiencing my surroundings; I'm not stopping to smell the roses.

Although I am generally optimistic, I'm a worrier and often have to remind myself not to worry about things I cannot control. What's done is done; learn from past mistakes, but do not dwell on them. Prepare yourself for future events, but don't worry about what might go wrong. A good example is something most of us dread – making a speech. If you think you have offended someone during a speech you have made, make a mental note not to do it again, but there's no point in mulling over something you cannot undo. There is also no point in mulling over the myriad of things that could go wrong with the speech you still have to make. Be well prepared, learn from past mistakes and try to relax in the present and think about what you're saying – chances are your speech will then be much better.

Happiness

With good health, love, wealth and the right attitude, happiness is inevitable. Unfortunately, any of the first three pillars can be toppled by events beyond our control. However we do have some control over the building, maintaining and rebuilding of these pillars and a lot of control over the fourth pillar of happiness – our attitude, which can help us find some happiness even when things seem to be going wrong.

I made the following prophetic diary entry at the ripe old age of twenty something:

"The worst thing about growing older is the way that doors keep closing around you. As a child you can dream of becoming a game ranger, a train driver, a vet, a race car driver or whatsoever else appeals to the mood of the moment. Those doors have not yet been closed by reality or attitude. You do not yet know that you will prefer living in the city to the country; that you will want more social status than the train driver; that you do not have the scientific aptitude to become a vet and that the opportunity to drive a race car will not come your way. It is only as you grow older that you discover that the selection of possibilities is determined more by chance than by choice. As doors begin to close, you realise that it is already too late to do some of the things you wanted to do; that you are proceeding to a point when it will be too late to do anything other than what you have done; and that you may well not leave the mark on history that you were once so sure you would!"

This sort of realisation leads us to the notion that we should seize the day (Carpe Diem)! "Twenty years from now you will be more disappointed by the things that you didn't do than by the ones you did do. So throw off the bowlines. Sail away from the safe harbour. Catch the trade winds in your sails. Explore. Dream. Discover" (Mark Twain). I certainly regret more the things I didn't do than the things I did. Although I have tried most sports and pastimes, I regret the fact that I have never tried surfing, nor driving a rally or race car, nor learned to pilot an aircraft. On the other hand, although long distance running has messed up my knees, I certainly do not regret running the Comrades ultra-marathon; in fact, it is one of my proudest achievements. I also have no regrets about sometimes overstretching my budget to buy things I really wanted and enjoyed; in particular some of the cars and boats I have owned or shared.

I do regret the many times my actions or words have hurt others, but regret more the hurt I've caused by inaction or lack of response. Of course, I regret the sad or bad things that have happened to me, like the early death of my father and my divorce. But the problem with the concept of regret in this sort of context is that you do not know how things would have turned out if the sad or bad things did not happen when they did. Had my father not died when he did and the whole family moved to South America, the rest of my life would have been very different from what I have experienced, and of course, I will never know whether it would have been better or worse. Had my divorce not have happened, I would not have ended up married to the woman I regard as my true soul mate.

Attractive as it may appear to "enjoy today and let tomorrow take care of itself" (Unknown), it is necessary to draw a line. If you "live like there's no tomorrow" (Omar Khayyam), there may well be no tomorrow or you may regret it when tomorrow comes. It is all very well to eat, drink and be merry today, but if you take stupid risks or fail to look after your health, tomorrow may not come at all. Even if it does, if you have spent all your money, hurt others, made a fool of yourself or even just have a bad hangover, tomorrow is not going to be much fun. I believe that it is a matter of finding the right balance. One of my mottoes used to be: "everything in moderation", but I have come to realise that even that needs to be modified. Perhaps "everything legal and reasonably sensible in moderation."

Chapter 13
Looking Forward

As I get nearer to the biblical lifespan of "three score years and ten", thoughts of illness and death are inevitable. I do, however, believe in the adage that "seventy is the new sixty". That, in terms of lifespan and lifestyle, my generation, at any given age, are the equivalent of ten years younger than my parents' generation.

Something that is of real concern to me is not being allowed to die with dignity. I firmly believe that life should not be prolonged if quality has gone and there is no hope of recovery. For this reason, my wife and I have Living Wills. For those not familiar with the concept of a Living Will, it is a directive made while the maker is of sound mind and which is considered to be legally binding on family, medical practitioners and health authorities, even if the maker is no longer able to take part in decisions about his/her future. It is to the effect that if there is no reasonable prospect of the maker recovering from severe physical or mental illness or impairment, he/she does not consent to the prolonging of the dying process by artificial means, nor to tube-feeding or resuscitation. The maker also asks to receive whatever quantity of drugs may be required to keep him/her free from pain or distress even if that hastens the moment of death.

Although Living Wills are not specifically recognised in South African law, legal opinion is that they are legally binding because no medical treatment may be provided to a patient without his/her informed consent. In the case of a Living Will, this consent is withdrawn in advance in stipulated circumstances. Euthanasia (the bringing about of death) is, however, illegal, even in such circumstances. So, although we can choose to have a pet put down to end its suffering, we cannot make the same choice for a loved one or even for ourselves. Although committing or attempting suicide is not illegal, a terminally ill patient would generally be unable to access any means to do so without assistance. Assisted suicide is illegal; in fact, it has been held in at least one South African case to constitute murder.

Sean Davison, a professor at the University of the Western Cape, while visiting his mother in New Zealand, assisted her to die by administering a lethal dose of morphine. His mother was eighty-four years old, had been a psychiatrist and remained of sound mind. However, she was dying from cancer. She had a Living Will and had tried to persuade her doctor and a friend to help to end her suffering. She was trying to starve herself to death and, after she had pleaded with her son, he complied with her wishes. After his "crime" was brought to the attention of the police by his sister, he was sentenced to five months house arrest in New Zealand for "procuring and counselling assisted suicide." Davison has subsequently returned to South Africa and founded the organisation Dignity South Africa, which aims to inform the public about the positive side of euthanasia and to seek a change in SA law.

In April, 2015, Robin Stransham-Ford, who studied law at the University of Rhodesia at the same time as I did and went on to become an advocate at the Cape Bar, was dying of prostate cancer. With the support of Dignity SA, he brought a successful High Court action against the Minister of Justice and others for the right to end his life with the assistance of a doctor. However, he died unassisted the day after the Judge's order without hearing of the Court's ruling. The State appealed against this ruling and, unfortunately, the Supreme Court of Appeal has just overturned the High Court ruling. At this stage, it is not clear what will happen next. Other places around the world are legalising assisted dying, but we appear to have taken a step backwards. Dignity SA are considering taking the matter to our Constitutional Court.

Thinking about death leads on to thoughts about religion, and in particular, whether or not there is an after-life and, if so, what it entails.

Is There a God?

I believe in God, to the extent that I say a silent prayer most nights before getting into bed. I start with the Lord's Prayer because it seems to me that it pretty much says it all. Then I add a few blessings, thanks and pleas, which I have standardised over the years. Sometimes, if I am particularly worried about one or more things, I will add some special pleas, which, in the more extreme cases, are repeated at various times during the day.

As most religions acknowledge, however, belief in God is a matter of faith as there is no empirical proof of his existence. Perhaps my belief in God is no more than wishful thinking. I want to believe in a god and in an after-life as these seem to make more sense of our life on earth. Surely there is some purpose to our relatively short lives? Given the incredible diversity of the natural world on earth – millions of species of animals, birds, reptiles, fish, insects, trees, flowers, grasses and so on in an amazing array of sizes, shapes and colours, living in forests, mountains, oceans, rivers, deserts, ice and snow-surely there must be some purpose to it all, some bigger plan? Add to that the fact that the earth is one small planet in a massive universe and that there are countless universes beyond our universe. How can we think we are at the centre even of our own universe, that we are the only intelligent beings or that it is all just a fluke of nature?

Perhaps the strongest motivator to belief is that we hope to be reunited with our loved ones who have died; surely they have not just gone forever?

Faith in Christianity?

I was baptised and confirmed in the Christian faith as a Presbyterian, but I am not a practising Christian in the sense of attending church and I do not accept all the teachings of Christianity. The first thing that challenged my faith was when, as a child, my beloved cat died and I asked my mother whether it would go to heaven. She suggested I ask our minister and he said no, only people go to heaven. I remember saying to my mother that wasn't fair and that if that was the way things work, I also didn't want to go to heaven.

Heaven or Hell?

The next thing to challenge my faith in Christian teachings was the death of my father, at the age of forty-five when I was only fourteen. My father was brought up as a Presbyterian but became an agnostic, and, given his experiences, I would not have been surprised if he had become an atheist. He spent the last couple of years of the Second World War in Japanese prisoner of war camps, and, like many POWs whose memoirs I have read, he must often have asked himself how any god could allow the kind of suffering to which they were exposed. When another minister told me that, unless my father had repented and found Jesus before he died (which I do not believe he had), he could not have gone to heaven, I could not accept that, and started questioning the teachings of Christianity more closely.

The biggest problem I have is with this concept that you cannot get to heaven except through Jesus; that your deeds on earth count for nought unless you have found Jesus and been "saved." Equally problematic for me is the linked concept that in the after-life you either go to heaven or you're doomed to eternal hell.

This means that only a relatively small number of born-again Christians can get to heaven and Jews, Hindus, Muslims, agnostics, atheists and all others are going to hell. No account is taken of relative opportunity. Obviously, someone born into a devout Christian family is much more likely to find Jesus than someone born into any other type of family. Also, the outcome is unrelated to how good or bad the individuals were during their lifetimes. As long as the Christians repented for their sins, no matter how bad, and even if only on their deathbeds, they get the ultimate reward. All the rest, no matter how devout in their own faiths and how good their deeds, get the ultimate punishment. I cannot believe that a just God would allow, let alone create, such an unjust system. Even our flawed criminal justice system on earth is fairer than this. You are judged on your actions not your beliefs and, even if you are convicted of a serious crime, you are not generally thrown into jail for the rest of your life. Punishment is related to the seriousness of the offence and takes into account a wide range of factors, including remorse. It is not all or nothing.

Attending Church?

I also have a problem with the way Christian church services are conducted. Being read to and preached at might have been necessary in times when most of the congregation could not read and, perhaps, were less able to think for themselves. But I find it frustrating to have to sit and listen to one person's interpretation of passages from the Bible and their applicability to modern life. From time to time, I find myself strongly disagreeing with what is being said, but there is no opportunity to ask questions or raise arguments. Saying prayers by rote and singing old-fashioned hymns also don't do anything for me.

When the time came for my younger son to be baptised, my then wife and I went to the local Presbyterian Church (at which we had attended a wedding and a couple of services) and spoke to the minister. I explained that I had been baptised and confirmed as a Presbyterian but was no longer a regular churchgoer; however, I wanted my son to have the same opportunity to be exposed to Christianity so that in due course he could make up his own mind. The minister was only prepared to baptise my son on condition that my wife and I attended church services on six consecutive Sundays before the baptism. We agreed to this and duly attended. I listened attentively to everything and tried without success to find meaning enough to warrant my continued attendance. The minister was surprised and no doubt very disappointed when I explained this to him.

No Justice on Earth?

Why do some babies die in the womb and other people live for over one hundred years? Why are some born with physical or mental defects or into poverty or abuse, while others are perfect specimens and have every opportunity in life? Why do evil people like President Robert Mugabe of Zimbabwe get to amass huge wealth and live to a ripe old age while many good people live in poverty and die young? Why are many species of animals being poached to extinction? Why do natural disasters like tsunamis and hurricanes wipe out whole communities? Why are man-made disasters like 9/11 in New York allowed to happen? If, as we are told, God is omnipotent and is a kind and loving God, surely all this injustice would not prevail?

I am not convinced by the answers given by Christians or followers of other religions I have heard. If mankind is being punished for general sin, why is the punishment so unevenly applied? If there is a purpose to everything and God has his reasons, why can't we get some explanations? If justice will prevail once we (or the fortunate few) get to heaven, what is the purpose of our time on earth? If we're being tested, why are some put through much more rigorous tests than others?

To my mind, a more rational answer to these questions is the old-fashioned belief that God is not omnipotent; that there is a devil, an evil spirit, whose will can sometimes overpower that of God. But that belief is closely linked to the concept of heaven and hell, with which I have already explained the problems I have. If the devil can cause suffering on earth, what prevents him causing suffering in the afterlife? What guarantee is there that the saved or good won't end up in hell?

Justice in the Afterlife?

Assuming there is an afterlife and it is not a simple matter of heaven or hell, what can we expect? Christians will tell you that the concepts of heaven and hell are beyond man's comprehension or even imagination; at the same time they will conjure up images of angels dressed in white, playing harps and floating on clouds (for heaven) and of demons dressed in black, torturing lost souls in fiery dungeons (for hell). Whilst that concept of hell is certainly unattractive, that concept of heaven also holds little attraction. Reminds me of the old joke: "I want to go to hell because that is where the bad girls go".

My concept of the afterlife is based on what I would like to find, on how I think things should be. First and foremost, I envisage the afterlife to involve a progression on a scale which ranges from ultimate unhappiness (despair or hell) through to ultimate happiness (bliss or heaven). Where you would start on that scale, and how long the progression would take, would depend on a complete range of factors relating to your life on earth: your opportunities, actions, omissions, beliefs etc.

Something which concerned me as a child about the afterlife is how someone like my late father would feel about having to wait for many years to be reunited with his loved ones. I came up with two solutions: first, that he could from time to time look down and see what we were doing on earth (not always an appealing notion from my point of view)! And second, that there is no concept of time in the afterlife, at least not in the sense that we experience time on earth – because time on earth is finite whereas time in the afterlife is infinite.

Another concern was how we would react to one another in the afterlife. Would my father see me as a fourteen-year-old or as an adult? Would I see him as a forty-five-year-old father figure or someone younger than me if I had died at a more advanced age? How would my father get on with my mother and her second husband? Again, I came up with some solutions. First, I do not think we retain a physical form or mental age in the afterlife but recognise one another on some spiritual level. I also think that we would be able to relate to one another on a completely different plane from that on earth: communicating at a fundamental level devoid of emotions like jealousy. Perhaps happiness will be derived from being able to communicate with whomever we choose, whenever and wherever we choose; even to relive happy times on earth. Maybe even to do some of the things we did not have the opportunity to do on earth, like drive a race car!

Conclusion

I want to live for as long as I have quality of life. While I certainly do not want to die, I do not fear death because as I see it, I will either go to a better place or I will altogether cease to exist. For that reason, I do not truly feel sorry for people who die, only for those they leave behind.

My notions of life after death may be way off the mark, but (here I'm going to make a huge and controversial claim), I believe they have a sounder basis in both logic and justice than the teachings of Christianity.

Chapter 14
Today

I recently reached an important milestone – what has for many years been the official retirement age for men: sixty-five. The fact is that I have already been semi-retired for a little over ten years, and, given my belief that sixty-five is the new fifty-five, I hope to have another ten years before I move into full retirement. I have decided that this would be an appropriate time to finish my *auto*biography.

At the time of writing this, Sherryl and I are still living happily in Johannesburg, South Africa. We have lots of plans and plenty to look forward to, and I hope and pray for more ups than downs as I head into my late sixties.

In regard to motor vehicles, I am happy with what I have: the Toyota Fortuner D4D for practicality and the Porsche Boxster S for fun. I find it difficult to understand the current trend to go for fast SUVs like the BMW X6, the Range Rover Sport and the Porsche Cayenne, which seem to me to fall between two stools – being neither proper sports cars nor proper off-roaders. Should I win the Lotto, I would probably replace my Fortuner with a new one and my Porsche with something more striking – probably a Ferrari or Lamborghini (if I could find one I could fit into comfortably) or possibly the BMW i8, which I saw for the first time a few months ago, or maybe the F-Type Jaguar or the stunning Porsche 918 Spyder or the Honda NSX. Perhaps more than one – nice to dream! Having visited the SA Festival of Motoring since writing about my dream cars, I need to make some changes. Sadly take out the BMW i8; although it looks great, the gullwing doors would make it impossible to park in the garage at home and difficult to park elsewhere, and the high side sills make it difficult to get in and out. Despite previously saying I would not buy another Audi, definitely add in the Audi R8 Plus, which appears to tick all the boxes.

Who knows what happens next?

JOHANNESBURG January 2017